THE SENSE
OF
RELIGIOUS
WONDER

Epistemological Variations

THE SENSE
OF
RELIGIOUS
WONDER

Epistemological Variations

by

Bernard J. Verkamp

SCRANTON: THE UNIVERSITY OF SCRANTON PRESS

© 2002 By The University of Scranton Press

Library of Congress Cataloging-in-Publication Data

Verkamp, Bernard J. (Bernard Joseph), 1938–
 The sense of religious wonder : epistemological variations / by Bernard J. Verkamp.
  p.cm.
 Includes bibliographical references and index.
 ISBN 1-58966-011-0 – ISBN 1-58966-003-X (pb.)
 1. Mystery. 2. Experience (Religion). 3. Knowledge, Theory of (Religion). I. Title.

BT127.5 . V48 2002
291.4'2–dc21   2002067270

Distribution:

University of Scranton Press
Chicago Distribution Center
11030 S. Langley
Chicago   IL   60628

PRINTED IN THE UNITED STATES OF AMERICA

For

David Cockerham

If one find friend with whom to fare,
Rapt in the well-abiding, apt,
Surmounting dangers one and all,
With joy fare with him mindfully.

— "The Rhinoceros," Sutta Nipata

CONTENTS

INTRODUCTION

In an earlier study, entitled *Senses of Mystery*, I tried to differentiate a religious sense of mystery from one that is purely natural by tracing how the object of the former experience has been interpreted variously down through the centuries as something more, in the sense of being either totally other than, immanent within, or transcendent to nature. Here, I will be concentrating more on the subjective side of the religious sense of mystery. In the process, questions will inevitably surface again about the nature of the mysterious object, and it will be seen how the latter has often been described in terms of Being, Wholeness, etc. But the primary concern will be to examine certain aspects of what a religious sense of mystery involves on the part of the person experiencing it. As Joachim Wach and others have previously noted, any religious experience will consist of at least three dimensions: the theoretical, the practical, and the social.[1] The concern here will only be with the first of these dimensions. While recognizing, therefore, that any individual encountering the mystery of reality in a religious way will sense a certain impetus both to action of a liturgical or moral sort as well as to the building of social relationships with God and man, the present study will be limited to an investigation of the theoretical side of the religious experience, and that only insofar as it pertains to one aspect of the cognitive dimension of such an experience. As important as the nature of religious language, or its component elements of symbolism, mythology, scriptures, creeds, theologies, and so forth, may be, little will be said about them in this study. Nor will we be trying to probe in any depth the role of reason in providing religious faith with a rational foundation for grasping in a conceptual way the mysterious object of religious experience. The focus rather will be on that most fundamental level of cognitive response evoked by a religious encounter with the mystery of reality, or, in other words, on what might be called the religious *sense*.

Among the many connotations of the English term *sense*, the most common probably is that of a faculty by which conscious animate beings are able to perceive certain aspects of reality. Many of the writers referred to in the following pages will speak of the religious sense of mystery in precisely such terms, namely, as a faculty by which humans are able to become aware of certain dimensions of reality that have not yet, or may never, be comprehended in a conceptual way. But such talk immediately gives rise to several questions.

In the first place, there arises a question about what exactly is meant by a faculty? Late eighteenth century proponents of the so-called faculty psychology had come to treat the faculties as though they were independent, substantial entities existing inside the human psyche like some *homunculus* that causes individuals to perform certain actions.[2] When no empirical evidence of such entities could be found, modern positivists were quick to dismiss all talk of such faculties as being nonsensical, a remnant of medieval superstition.[3] It could be argued, however, that the faculty psychologists had completely distorted what Thomas Aquinas and other medieval philosophers had meant by a faculty. Following the lead of Aristotle, the medieval thinkers had really intended a faculty to be understood as a potency or, in other words, as a disposition of a being to acquire a certain perfection to perform a certain action.[4] Such a potency, they said, is passive when it refers to the capacity of a being to become or do something that is not inherent to its nature. They often used the term in this passive sense to refer to the receptivity of human beings toward elevation by divine grace onto a higher level of being, or to the aptitude of human nature for hypostatic union, or of material objects for sacramental use.[5] But they also spoke of a potency as being active when referring to the innate disposition or ability of a being to become or do something in accord with its own nature.[6] Understood in this medieval sense of an active potency, the term faculty may not be all that foreign to what modern thinkers are saying about the modularity of the human mind, or about its natural tendencies to act in one way or another.[7] In any event, it is in some such general sense that the thinkers referred to in the following pages will try to describe the religious sense of mystery. In one way or another, all of them will say that having a religious sense of mystery means, among other things, to enjoy some special tendency or ability by which to experience the mysterious dimensions of reality.

Secondly, identification of the religious sense as a faculty raises a question about what such a faculty might consist of, or, in other words, what kind of faculty it might be said to be. More often than not, the English word *sense* has been used to describe the special faculties connected with physical organs (eyes, ears, etc.) by which animals, including humans, are able to see, hear, smell, taste, and touch certain aspects of the external world, such as color, sound, odor, flavor, warmth, etc. But the word has frequently been used also to denote faculties of another sort. Medieval philosophers, for example, spoke of certain internal senses, among which, in addition to the imagination, memory, and cogitative power, they counted especially the so-called central sense, by which the human mind is enabled to do what the external senses cannot do either individually or collectively, and that is "to combine sensations into total sensory awareness [i.e., a 'perception'] of a present object."[8]

More recently, Cardinal Newman referred to the ability of the human mind to detect the holistic meaning of any given field of evidence as an illative sense,[9] and compared it to other uses of the term to describe the various faculties by which humans discern the beauty of their world (the aesthetic sense), the difference between right and wrong (the moral sense), the amusing side of life (the sense of humor), etc.[10] Use of the term in such a way presupposes, as John Baillie has pointed out, that "the human spirit . . . develops certain subtler senses or sensitivities which go beyond the bodily senses," and make us "sensitive to aspects of reality of which [the bodily senses], taken by themselves, could not conceivably inform us."[11] And that is precisely what most of the thinkers referred to in subsequent chapters of this book (including Baillie himself) assume when they talk of a religious sense of mystery. While readily admitting that any such sense will to some extent involve the external senses, they will also deny that the latter, on their own, and prior to any operation of the human intellect, can deliver any genuinely religious experience of the mysterious dimensions of reality. In brief, they have in mind a kind of faculty that facilitates the religious experience of mystery through the cooperation of the human intellect and the external senses. How exactly such cooperation is to be explained, however, is another question, to which a variety of answers will be given, depending upon how one or another thinker interprets the relation of body/brain to soul/mind. And the answer given to this question will in turn largely determine whether the religious sense or faculty is interpreted as an instinct, a cognitive disposition, an emotive proclivity, a cogitative power, or some combination thereof.

The English term *sense* can also be used, it should be noted, to refer to the perception, awareness, apprehension, and/or feeling resulting from the actualization or exercise of one or another potency or faculty.

And that is the case with the religious sense of mystery also. Those who speak of the latter will generally have in mind not only the faculty by which humans are enabled to experience the mystery of reality, but also the perceptive awareness and/or feeling resulting therefrom. These terms, however, are themselves quite ambiguous, with much debate occurring within philosophical and psychological circles about what exactly constitutes the nature of perception and feeling, or how either or both of them might be said to enjoy a cognitive dimension. Close attention will also need to be given, therefore, to what exactly is meant when the thinkers referred to in the following pages speak, as they do, of the religious sense in terms of a perceptual or emotive form of awareness. Ideally, perhaps, their discussion in this regard might best have been presented by separating the book into two sections: one dealing with the potency or faculty, the other with its actualization. But most of the thinkers intermingle their discussion of both aspects to such an extent that it would be nearly impossible, or at least highly repetitive, to treat what they say in one respect apart from what they say about the other. Accordingly, I will be dealing with both aspects within the single context of their respective, overall theories about the religious sense of mystery.

At least five different ways of conceiving of the religious sense are reviewed in the chapters that follow. Multiple variations on each might have been added. But my concern was not to provide an exhaustive list of every conceivable theory, but simply to indicate some of the broader frames of reference within which such variations have been developed in the past. Nor has there been any attempt to harmonize all the various lines of thought reviewed. To have tried would only have served to confuse matters more than they already are. The different views, therefore, will each be presented on their own terms, and the reader can decide for him or herself which best captures the phenomenon under discussion. This is not to say, of course, that there is no common ground between them. And in the concluding chapter of this book I will try to pull together some of the major emphases shared by all the different theories.

Finally, it should be noted from the start that the present study will be limited to those interpretations of religion which take the experience of mystery seriously as a positive response to reality. Theories by the likes of Ludwig Feuerbach, Karl Marx, Friedrich Nietzsche, Sigmund Freud, and others, who, as noted in my earlier study on the *Senses of Mystery*, reject the view that there is anything ultimately mysterious about reality, and who, therefore, dismiss oceanic feeling, the sympathy of the whole, or any other religious sense of mystery as being nothing more than a neurotic exercise in wishful thinking, or the projection of an alienated self, will, for all their significance, receive only passing notice here.

NOTES

[1] See Joachim Wach, *Sociology of Religion* (Chicago and London: The University of Chicago, 1967), 17–34.

[2] See James E. Royce, *Man and Meaning* (New York: McGraw-Hill, Inc., 1969), 58, 195; *NCE* 5:635; *Dictionary of Philosophy and Psychology*, edited by James Mark Baldwin (Gloucester, MA: Peter Smith, 1960), I: 369.

[3] See *NCE* 11:635.

[4] See *NCE* 5:788–789; 11:633.

[5] See *NCE* 11:634; Peter A. Angeles, *Dictionary of Philosophy* (New York: Harper and Row, 1981), 219.

[6] See *NCE* 11:634; Angeles, *Dictionary*, 219.

[7] See Royce, *Man and Meaning*, 195; *Oxford Companion of the Mind*, edited by Richard L. Gregory (Oxford, New York: Oxford University Press, 1987), 253–254.

[8] See Royce, *Man and Meaning*, 65; *NCE* 13:92.

[9] John Henry Newman, *Grammar of Assent* (Garden City, NY: Doubleday and Company, Inc., 1955), 270–299; see also: John Hick, *Faith and Knowledge* (Ithaca and London: Cornell University Press, 1970), 81.

[10] Newman, *Grammar*, 271; see also: John Baillie, *The Sense of the Presence of God* (New York: Charles Scribner's Sons, 1962), 52–53.

[11] Baillie, Presence of God, 52–53.

CHAPTER ONE

Biological Instinct/ Genetic Propensity

One way to interpret the religious *sense* of mystery as a faculty by which religious people experience the mystery of reality would be to define it as an instinct, or to say that such a religious sense has at least an instinctive base.

That lower animals, and especially insects such as bees and ants, are subject to instinct has long been assumed. Throughout the Middle Ages, for example, many Aristotelian thinkers, anticipating or following Avicenna's reading of Aristotle's suggestion that "animals know by nature,"[1] had tried to explain certain patterns of animal behavior, such as the lamb's flight from the wolf, as the result of that animal's soul having been infused by God with a certain estimative power, by which it could "know concretely" what was "suitable" or "harmful" to its survival.[2] While admitting that the animal had no conceptual knowledge of good and evil, it was argued that by virtue of the estimative power it could have an innate awareness of concrete, individualized goods, and that this knowledge could generate desire that would in turn incline the animal to seek that which is of advantage to its own survival or that of the species.[3] With the exception of the Behaviorists, who were intent upon explaining animal behavior as the result of operant conditioning alone, without any recourse to instinct,[4] a majority of modern scientists spurred on by the work of ethologists such as Nicholas Tinbergen and Konrad Lorenz[5] have assumed that instinct is a major factor in the animal kingdom,[6] and have generally understood such instinct to refer to an innate impulse, drive, or propensity, on the part of all members of an animal species to act in a uniform, immediately perfect, constant, and specialized way, toward the achievement of some adaptive goal, such as

1

the building of a nest, with some dim and vague, emotive/appetitive awareness of the particular action being performed and the pleasure to be derived therefrom, but without any previous experiential training, rational deliberation, or foresight of the goal being pursued.[7]

Among the instincts attributed by past thinkers to lower animals, some have been said to be of a religious nature. The devotion of a dog to its master, the ritualistic rain dancing performed by some primates, or the ritual flight patterns of flocks of birds in the sky, along with other types of instinctive animal behavior, have been said by Charles Darwin, Alister Hardy, Alfred North Whitehead, and others to have anticipated man's own religious activity.[8] The seventeenth century Cambridge Platonist, Henry More, even went so far as to suggest that animals can experience the same cognitive feeling of wonder that is generally associated with the religious sense of mystery on the part of man. "At the sight of the sun or moon," More wrote, apes and elephants display a "strange sense or impress," and their subsequent behavior indicate[s] that these animals experience "Love, Fear and Wonderment, near to that Passion which in us is called Veneration."[9] The early twentieth century American psychologist William McDougall would similarly attribute to animals an "instinct of curiosity."[10] But he would also observe that in brute animals, such an instinctively emotive response never goes beyond what Rene Descartes called "astonishment,"[11] in that it "merely serves to rivet [the animal's] attention upon unfamiliar objects," and involves no awareness of a lack of knowledge or a desire to learn such as will be seen to characterize the human experience of wonder.[12] Underlying such a conclusion was the Cartesian assumption that animal instinct is altogether blind, without "the least stirrings of intelligence or reason."[13] Not everyone, of course, including many of the thinkers referred to later in this chapter, would agree that animal and human ways of knowing are so radically different, and on that account would be inclined to see any human religious instinct as being nothing more than a relatively more sophisticated version of the instinct of curiosity, ritual, and so forth, found among the lower animals. But if the assumption is made that human intelligence differs in kind, and not merely by degree, then there is reason to conclude that whatever rudiments of religious instinct are to be found among animals lower than man, they have undergone radical modification upon coming under the influence of human reason, and that the human instinct of wonder is of a radically different sort from whatever emotion it is that is aroused by the animal instinct of curiosity.

But are humans subject to instinct of any sort? Already in the medieval discussion of the estimative power it had been argued that during at least the earliest years of human life, when reason and learning are not yet sufficient for guiding behavior, the child has to rely on the primitive cognition afforded by the estimative power.[14] But after the child achieves the use of reason, its estimative power was said to become either "unimportant,"[15] or, as Thomas Aquinas, following Averroes, claimed, radically altered into a cogitative power,[16] which as we shall see in a subsequent chapter,[17] can only be appreciated in the context of what Thomas said about the intimate union of body and soul in man, and as a power, therefore, that is of a radically different sort from what is generally understood by instinct. Later, in the seventeenth century, Descartes, Lord Herbert of Cherbury, many of the Cambridge Platonists, G. W. von Leibniz, and a host of other thinkers would speak of a Natural Light or Natural Instinct guiding human behavior.[18] But in their view, such instinct was of a spiritual, rather than a biological, sort, and to that extent might better be discussed in our later examination of some of the Rationalistic interpretations of the religious sense of mystery. Under the influence of Charles Darwin and Herbert Spencer,[19] however, discussion of the role of instinct in human behavior along more Naturalistic lines would carry over into the present century. Especially noteworthy in this regard were two Harvard psychologists, William James and William McDougall.

James, who by his own admission had a naturalistic view of religion to the extent of acknowledging that all the forms of thought operative in the realm of religion have a *natural* origin,[20] claimed that far from having fewer instincts than the brutes, man is actually "more richly endowed in this respect than any other mammal."[21] Defining instinct as "the faculty of acting in such a way as to produce certain ends, without foresight of the ends, and without previous education in the performance,"[22] James identified at least thirty special instincts to which humans are subject.[23] Some Naturalistic interpreters of religion, however, have tried to support their own view of the religious sense as being nothing more than an acquired habit, by claiming that James "assert[ed] categorically that there is no religious instinct in man."[24] And in one sense they are right. For it is certainly true that according to James the "religious sentiment . . . contains nothing whatever of a psychologically specific nature."[25] Religious fear, love, awe, joy, and so forth, he says, are simply "man's natural emotion[s] . . . directed to a religious object."[26] There thus seems to be, he continues, "no one elementary religious emotion, but only a common storehouse of emotions upon which religious objects may draw."[27] Such passages would seem to imply that there is no specifically religious instinct, and as a matter of fact, James does not include any such item in his list of special human instincts. But this need not be taken to mean that he rejected an instinctive base to the religious sentiment. That he did not is suggested, in the first place, by the fact that James eventually came to understand emotion as "a direct response to the instinctive wisdom of the body."[28] When, therefore, he speaks of religious objects drawing upon "a common storehouse of *emotions*," he is as much as saying that religious objects draw upon "a common storehouse of *instincts*." Whatever cognitive dimension there is to the religious sentiment, in other words, it derives from the meaning of instinctive bodily reactions.[29] Furthermore, as Robert Richards has noted,[30] James moved steadily throughout his life toward a more "nativistic conception of the human mind," increasingly recognizing an "organic structure" of the mind to account for not only the so-called "necessary truths," but also "our emotional and instinctive tendencies."[31] Not only did he come to reject as absurd the empiricist claim that aesthetic, ethical, and presumably religious ways of "relating" the data of experience could be accounted for exclusively by the experience of the individual, he also dismissed any "evolutionary empiricism," such as that propounded by Herbert Spencer, according to which the "organic structure of the mind" might be attributed "not to the experience of the individual, but to that of his ancestors as far back as one may please to go."[32] Finally, it may be noted, that like his fellow pragmatist, Charles S. Peirce, James sometimes explicitly referred to the "instinctive" nature of the religious sentiment.[33]

When, therefore, James wrote that in our "human consciousness," in our "mental machinery," is to be found an "undifferentiated . . . sense of reality, a feeling of objective presence, a perception of what we may call 'something more,' more deep and more general than any of the special and particular 'senses' [can] yield,"[34] it is reasonable to assume that he was talking about an instinctive dimension of the religious experience. Rightly or wrongly, he clearly had in mind to suggest that such a religious sentiment of the more is independent of any kind of intellectual activity, and is, therefore, pre-conceptual, and because of its direct, dim, and inarticulate nature, closer, perhaps, to a sensation than to a thought process.[35] This should not be taken to mean, however, as some have, that according to James the religious sense is without any epistemic dimension. For, as we have already noted, James was of the view that there is a certain wisdom or meaning in the body's instinctive reactions. According to James, in other words, man knows instinctively that there is something more to reality than meets the eye—an "unseen order," an "ideal realm," the realm of the "divine."[36]

For McDougall too, instincts were something "more than innate tendencies or dispositions to certain kinds of movement."[37] "Every instance of instinctive behavior," he wrote, "has three aspects—the cognitive, the affective, and the connative; that is to say, [every instinct] involves a knowing of some thing or object, a feeling in regard to it, and a striving towards or away from that object."[38] An instinct may be defined, then, McDougall continued, as "an inherited or innate psycho-physical disposition which determines its possessor to perceive, and to pay attention to, objects of a certain class, to experience an emotional excitement of a particular quality upon perceiving such an object, and to act in regard to it in a particular manner, or, at least, to experience an impulse to such an action."[39] Correlative to the aforementioned three basic aspects of every instinct, McDougall then went on to say, are "three corresponding parts of the total disposition": corresponding to the affective aspect is the "central part," which controls the "distribution of the nervous impulses, especially . . . the working of the visceral organs"; corresponding to the connative aspect is the "efferent or motor part," which "determines the distribution of impulses to the muscles of the skeletal system by which the instinctive action is affected."[40] While the afferent and efferent parts may be modified by experience of environmental influences, the central part "remains unmodified."[41] "The emotional excitement," therefore, "with the accompanying nervous activities of the central part of the disposition, is the only part of the total instinctive process that retains its specific character and remains common to all individuals and all situations in which the instinct is excited."[42]

Although McDougall will sometimes refer in passing to what he calls a "religious instinct,"[43] more often than not he will, like James, only speak of an instinctive base to religion. The "instinct of subjection,"[44] the "instinct of fear,"[45] and a host of other instincts may all play a role, he says, but it is the "instinct of curiosity" which is most responsible for the initial generation of the "emotion of wonder,"[46] which along with its concomitant sentiments of admiration and awe, "must be regarded as one of the principal roots of both science and religion."[47] What excites curiosity on the part of both animals and humans, and triggers their rapidly alternating responses of "approach and retreat," McDougall claimed, is "any object similar to, yet perceptibly different from, familiar objects habitually noticed."[48] Such objects will vary, depending upon the experience of the individual, and so too will the response to them. In the animals, as noted earlier, "the instinct of curiosity . . . merely serves to rivet their attention upon unfamiliar objects," such as "disease and death, pestilence and famine, storm and flood, lightning and thunder, and the powerful beasts of prey," must have become "the objects of man's awful contemplation," and given rise to a variety of responses, including, climactically, the conception of spirits and divine powers.[49] But however much the cognitive and connative aspects of the instinct of curiosity might vary throughout the experience and interpretation of "unfamiliar objects," the affective aspect—the feeling of wonder—remains unchanged. As religion gradually evolved into higher levels of symbolic complexity, new instincts (e.g., subjection, parental) might have been triggered and given rise to other emotions (e.g., gratitude, awe, reverence). But "the leading part in the evolution of religion" remained the "instinct of curiosity" and its accompanying emotion of "wonder."[50]

Some of McDougall's contemporaries—for example William K. Wright of Cornell University—tried to apply his conclusions to the question about "the genesis of the categories" by suggesting that the religious category of "truth" has "a definite instinctive foundation . . . chiefly in the instinct of curiosity and its accompanying emotion of wonder."[51] Defining "truth" from a "pragmatist" perspective as a "socially created . . . category, by means of which we organize our perceptual and imaginal experience in order to accomplish our ends," Wright contended that the content of the judgments utilized by most individuals in their thinking is for the most part drawn from a "storehouse of accepted truths" that is "chiefly stocked with truths that in the first instance were the fruit of 'disinterested' curiosity . . . with reference to the free play of images and ideas."[52]

In subsequent decades, however, the tendency to multiply exponentially the number of human instincts, along with the seemingly circular, tautological nature of some of the arguments being propounded by those defending the role of instinct, caused some, and especially J. B. Watson, B. F. Skinner, and their fellow Behaviorists, to reject instinct altogether as a factor in human behavior, and to ascribe the latter entirely to the influence of experience and environment.[53] Typical of this behaviorist view was the suggestion made by J. J. Smith back in the 1940s to the effect that "the human being at birth is nonreligious in the same sense that he is nonscientific, nonmoral, or nonaesthetic," because "he inherits none of these qualities in a functional form but acquires them gradually through experience."[54] The complex system of concepts, emotions, desires, attitudes, and personality traits associated with religion is "built up" gradually and exclusively, he writes, under the influence of environmental factors such as the home, the school, and the church.[55] "The human being at birth," he concluded, "holds a neutral status as regards religion; the baby is neither religious nor antireligious."[56] Jean Piaget, whose views have dominated child psychology in recent decades, rejected such raw empiricism, on the grounds that it does not pay enough attention to the "active role of the subject."[57] Piaget himself, however, also denied that "the subject possesses from the start endogenous structures which it imposes on objects,"[58] and concluded instead that if there is anything innate in the human mind, it is only "certain modes of interacting with the environment," i.e., "adaptive" and "organizational functions."[59] Religious "structures," therefore, are interpreted by Piaget and disciples of his, such as Lawrence Kohlberg and James Fowler,[60] as being "constructed" out of the interaction of the subject and the environment—specifically, as Pierre Bovet had earlier suggested,[61] out of the child's transfer, at about the age of six, of parental "omnipotence" and "omniscience" onto the "gods" or "ideal figures" it has learned about in religious instruction.[62]

Such an anti-instinctivist trend was consistently resisted over the years, however, not only by the likes of Sigmund Freud and Konrad Lorenz, both of whom emphasized the role of instinct in the motivation of sex and aggression,[63] but more particularly in regard to religion by Freud's one time disciple, Carl Gustav Jung. Breaking with Freud, who conceived of the "unconscious" as the "gathering place of forgotten and repressed contents,"[64] Jung distinguished a "personal" and a "collective" unconscious, the former owing its existence to "personal experience," and consisting of contents which have disappeared from consciousness through having been forgotten or repressed, the latter deriving not from personal experience but being "inborn,"[65] and consisting of contents ("essentially the archetypes"[66]) that "have never been in consciousness, and therefore have never been individually acquired, but owe their existence exclusively to heredity."[67] It is "a great mistake," therefore, Jung wrote, "to suppose that the psyche of a newborn child is a *tabula rasa* in the sense that there is absolutely nothing in it."[68] The "preconscious psyche—for example, that of the newborn infant—is not an empty vessel into which, under favorable conditions, practically anything can be poured."[69] On the contrary, "the child is born with a differentiated brain that is predetermined by heredity."[70] To that extent, "it meets sensory stimuli coming from outside not with *any* aptitudes, but with *specific* ones, and this necessarily results in a particular, individual choice and pattern of apperception."[71] These aptitudes can be shown to be "inherited instincts and preformed patterns, the latter being the *a priori* and formal conditions of apperception that are based on instinct . . . they are the archetypes."[72]

Jung compared these archetypes not only to the Platonic Ideas, but also to what Lucien Levy-Bruhl called the "*representations collectives*" of primitive peoples, to what the Durkheimian scholars Henri Hubert and Marcel Mauss labeled, with reference to the Kantian categories, the "categories of imagination," or, finally, to what the ethnologist Adolf Bastian classified as "elementary ideas."[73] Whatever the basis for such comparisons,[74] it should be noted that Jung repeatedly insisted that he did not consider the archetypes "inherited ideas" or "definite mythological images."[75] The archetype, he claimed, is "empty and purely formal, nothing but a *facultas praeformandi*, a possibility of representation which is given *a priori*."[76] The "representations themselves are not inherited, only the forms, and in that respect they correspond in every way to the instincts"[77] They are an "instinctive trend, as marked as the impulse of birds to build nests, or ants to form organized colonies."[78] "Collective thought patterns of the human mind . . . innate and inherited," they are "not just static patterns," but "dynamic factors that manifest themselves in impulses,"[79] and "create myths, religions, and philosophies."[80] These archetypes "are not disseminated only by tradition, language, and migration,"[81] Jung contended. "They can rearise spontaneously, at any time, at any place, and without any outside influence."[82] They are "present always and everywhere."[83] They "emanate . . . from the unconscious," and "independent of tradition . . . guarantee in every single individual a similarity and even a sameness of experience, and also of the way it is represented imaginatively."[84] "When a situation occurs which corresponds to a given archetype, that archetype becomes activated and a compulsiveness appears, which, like an instinctual drive, gains its way against all reason and will, or else produces a conflict of pathological dimensions, that is to say a neurosis."[85] The "function" of these archetypes is "to compensate or correct . . . the inevitable one-sidedness and extravagances of the conscious mind"[86] by "uniting opposites" and "[mediating] between the unconscious substratum and the conscious mind."[87] That such archetypes do exist and are innate, Jung wrote, is evidenced by their universality.[88] This universality can be demonstrated, however, only to the extent that the archetypes "manifest themselves."[89] The method for proving the existence of archetypes, therefore, is to study the material (i.e., myths, dreams, fantasies, delusions, etc.) in which they do express themselves.[90]

Finally, it should be noted that while many life and social scientists today still seem reluctant to refer explicitly to the role of instinct in human behavior, many do nonetheless often posit biological and evolutionary constraints upon human learning,[91] and to that extent at least complement the instinctivist interpretation of the religious sense of mystery. A good example in this regard can be found in the so-called "sociobiology" founded by Edward O. Wilson and others back in the 1970s.

Underlying this supposed influence of biology on social culture is the operation of what Wilson, in collaboration with Charles Lumsden and others, refers to as an "epigenetic rule." By an "epigenetic rule," they say, is meant "any regularity during epigenesis [the total process of interaction between genes and environment] that channels the development of an anatomical, physiological, cognitive, or behavioral trait in a particular direction."[92] Some such "rules," such as the natural propensity of all human beings to perceive color in terms of four basic "categories" of "blue, green, yellow, and red,"[93] or the natural preference of humans for sweet, as opposed to sour tastes, are said to be "primary,"[94] in that they "are based upon the more automatic processes that lead from sensory filtering to perception."[95] Others are said to be "secondary," because they are thought to govern the way the perceived raw information (colors, etc.) is evaluated "through the processes of memory, emotional response, and decision making" so as to enhance the possibility of adaptive behavior.[96] The attachment of mothers to their newborn infants, the infantile fear of strangers, the avoidance of incest, and facial recognition are a few of the examples given by Wilson and Lumsden of the operation of such secondary epigenetic rules in the cognitive development of human beings.[97] They suggest, however, that with additional study, "many more epigenetic rules [primary as well as secondary] will come to light."[98]

Michael Ruse has followed up on that suggestion, and pointed out what he considers to be some good candidates. "Our minds," he writes, "are not *tabula rasae*. Rather, they are structured according to various innate dispositions [or rules], which have proven their worth in the past struggles of proto-humans." These dispositions "do not yield fully explicit, innate ideas; but, as we grow, triggered and informed by life's experiences, the dispositions incline us to think and act in various tried and trustworthy patterns."[99] Thus, for example, the raw material of science, he continues, is not only "filtered and transformed" in accordance with certain primary epigenetic rules, but its whole inductive/deductive methodology is governed by the operation of secondary epigenetic rules.[100] Studies of childhood development, cross-cultural consistencies, and ethological studies of higher primates, all suggest, he notes, that the human penchant for finding causal connections, the urge toward consilience, as well as the logical propensity to adhere to the law of non-contradiction or to the form of logical argumentation called *modus ponens*, are products of secondary epigenetic rules, "brought into existence by natural selection"—"no less than there is a rule setting up incest barriers."[101] Just as the discrimination of color and taste, or the avoidance of incest, provided our human ancestors with "clear adaptive advantage," so too did the secondary epigenetic rules that generated the aforementioned scientific principles.[102]

Hume, rather than Kant, should be considered the "philosophical precursor" of this Darwinian epistemology, Ruse argues, because the "propensities" recognized by Hume were said to incline the mind to see things in certain ways (e.g., causal connections) not because (as Kant thought) of any necessity in the nature of things, but because of the adaptive value or utility for preservation and propagation of the species.[103] Hume also must be considered the more "genuine precursor" of Darwinian ethics, since just as Kant "wanted a necessity to knowledge that Darwin forbids," so he "wanted a necessity to moral imperatives foreign to the modern evolutionists [e.g., the categorical imperative]."[104] More consistent with the thinking of Hume, evolutionary ethics, Ruse notes, makes no claim of necessity.[105] What it does claim is that "we have genetically based dispositions to approve of certain courses of action and to disapprove of other courses of action."[106] Thus, for example, natural selection, according to Ruse, has taken a "middle course" between "firm genetic control" (as seen in ant behavior) and "purely rational" decision making, and endowed us with "epigenetic rules" that incline us, but do not force us, to be altruistic.[107] "No one is claiming," Ruse cautions, "that every last moral twitch is tightly controlled by the genes,"[108] or that "every last act of Western man or woman is governed by kin selection or reciprocal altruism."[109] All that is being argued, he concludes, is that just as "in science . . . human reason has certain rough or broad constraints, as manifested through the epigenetic rules," so "in the case of ethics . . . human moral thought has constraints, as manifested through the epigenetic rules, and the application of these leads to moral codes, soaring from biology into culture."[110]

What about religion? Are there epigenetic rules of a religious sort? Might the religious sense of mystery be considered a product of natural selection, and based therefore upon a genetically endowed, innate propensity or disposition to envision reality in terms of mystery? Wilson himself seemed to think that it was. Inherent to the religious sense of mystery, at least to one of its variations (as described by Rudolf Otto, Mircea Eliade, and a host of other modern scholars of religion), is the "dichotomization of objects into sacred and profane." But according to Wilson, such a propensity for sacralization is only one of many elements of the religious phenomenon which functioned in the past "to circumscribe a social group and bind its members together in unquestioning allegiance."[111] Such forms of religious practice, he claimed, "can be seen to have [conferred] biological advantage," and genes favoring them to have been "strongly selected for" in the process of evolution.[112]

The conditions to which sacralization and other manifestations of the religious sense of mystery were adaptive may now be gone, and religion itself may give way to "scientific materialism,"[113] Wilson notes, but past societies practicing religion "have been much more likely to survive than those that did not."[114] Ruse draws a similar conclusion. Describing religion (and not only fundamentalism, with its so-called "creation-science," but also "the more conventional and respectable forms of religious belief") as "perhaps the most extreme form of nonscience," Ruse leaves little doubt that he shares Wilson's conviction that religion will give way increasingly to "scientific materialism."[115] But he also agrees with Wilson about the adaptive value of religion in the past.[116] How can this be? "If science is grounded in selection-produced epigenetic rules, and if evolutionary biology is as vital to humans as I say it is, then why is it that so many people embrace so enthusiastically a potpourri of nonscientific doctrines, from Catholicism to scientology?"[117] The answer, he suggests, is to be found in "the fact . . . that humans, like other organisms, are complex beings, balancing diverse interests and needs . . . to mesh with fellow humans, [etc.]."[118] "Quite clearly, therefore," Ruse concludes, "success in the struggle for survival and reproduction needs more than epigenetic rules about logic and science. It needs dispositions for the other aspects of the human experience."[119] The tendency to believe in a supreme being to resolve the mystery of evil, as exemplified in the Book of Job, may be one such disposition, "even though such belief may be blatantly anti-scientific."[120] Another may be our propensity to "wonder about the unseen and the unseeable." The "feeling of wonder" resulting there-from, Ruse notes, "clearly has its own adaptive value."[121] Religion, therefore, and its various senses of mystery, may be said to "stem from our biological nature as much as does science."[122]

Support for the views of Wilson and Ruse in this regard can be found in the work of the many other modern scientists and philosophers who have studied the brain and concluded that just as the nerve cells are genetically arranged to provide for "sets of potentialities" or "programs" that direct the achievement of "life-aims" such as walking, reading, speaking, recognition of faces, etc.,[123] so there are "coded lists of instructions" (i.e., "programs") of the brain that predispose human beings toward aesthetic experiences, altruistic behavior, and "other attitudes lying behind social organization, including commanding and obeying, believing, worshiping, and many more."[124] The brain may be "plastic" and subject to environmental influences as it strives toward the particular, detailed forms of culture,[125] but it is not a *tabula rasa*,[126] and perception is not a merely passive process.[127] Human perception is rather, they say, "an active search for information,"[128] facilitated by a brain that is genetically programed through a process of natural selectivity to be "purposive"[129] in a way that includes the metaphorical mapping of the holistic, mysterious boundaries of reality.[130]

Underlying the conclusions of some of the thinkers referred to in this chapter is the view that the human mind is either identical with the brain, or is nothing more than an epiphenomenon or function of it, and that the religious sense of mystery, therefore, can be reduced to one or another genetically determined brain state, or in other words, to nothing more than the product of a physiological, neurological process. But even if this naturalistic/materialistic prejudice is rejected—as it is by most of the thinkers we will be dealing with in subsequent chapters—and a real distinction is recognized between the mind and the brain on the basis of a more fundamental differentiation of soul and body, it might still be possible to acknowledge an instinctive dimension of the religious sense to the extent that any faculty of the soul or mind, whereby humans might, according to such thinkers, be able to sense the mystery of reality, is rooted in, built upon, and coordinated with the evolutionally programed body/brain in the actualization of its potentiality. How this could occur, and what it might say about the subjective nature of the religious sense of mystery, will be taken up in subsequent chapters.

NOTES

[1] See G. P. Klubertanz, "Estimative Power," *NCE* 5:558; G. P. Klubertanz, *The Discursive Power* (Saint Louis: The Modern Schoolman, 1952), 89–106. For a discussion of Aristotle and his commentators in this regard, see *Ibid.*, 18–89, 106–151.

[2] See, for example, Thomas Aquinas, *The Summa Theologica* 78.4, *GB* 19:411–413; Klubertanz, *The Discursive Power*, 152–161; 265–275. See also Robert J. Richards, "Influence of Sensationalist Tradition on Early Theories of the Evolution of Behavior," *Journal of the History of Ideas* 40 (1979):86.

[3] See Klubertanz, *The Discursive Power*, 160; *NCE* 5:558.

[4] See *IESS* 7:367, 370–371.

[5] For a good introduction, see Robert J. Richards, "The Innate and Learned: The Evolution of Konrad Lorenz's Theory of Instinct," *Philosophy of the Social Sciences* 4(1974): 131n.20; R. J. Richards, *Darwin and the Emergence of Evolutionary Theories of Mind and Behavior* (Chicago: The University of Chicago Press, 1987), 528–536; *IESS* 7: 367–369.

[6] See Richards, *Darwin*, index, 679–680.

[7] Although some modern thinkers have been inclined to describe instincts as being nothing more than reflex actions, most have followed the etymological connotation of the original Latin word for instinct (as being driven from within), and referred to instinct, therefore, as an impulse, drive, or propensity (see W. H. Thorpe, *Learning and Instinct in Animals* [London: Methuen and Co., 1956],15). For a brief introduction on all these points, see *IESS* 7:363–371: J. F. Donceel, *Philosophical Anthropology* (New York: Sheed and Ward, 1967), 92.

[8] See Bernard J. Verkamp, *The Evolution of Religion: A Re-examination* (Scranton: The University of Scranton Press, 1995), 23–26.

[9] See Peter Harrison, *Religion and the Religions in the English Enlightenment* (Cambridge: Cambridge University Press, 1990), 44–45.

[10] William McDougall, *An Introduction to Social Psychology* (Boston: John W. Luce and Co., 1926), 310–312.

[11] Rene Descartes, *The Passions of the Soul* (Indianapolis/Cambridge: Hackett Publishing Company, 1989), 58–59, 60.

[12] McDougall, *Social Psychology*, 310.

[13] As cited in Richards, "Influence," 86.

[14] See *NCE* 5:558; 3:981.

[15] Klubertanz, *Discursive Power*, 276.

[16] *Ibid.*, 161–264, esp., 276; *NCE* 3:980–982.

[17] See *Infra*, Chapter Four.

[18] See *Infra*, Chapter Two.

[19] See Richards, *Darwin*, 83–124, 283–286.

[20] William James, *Principles of Psychology*, *GB* 53: 53, 851, 859.

[21] *Ibid.*, 704.

[22] *Ibid.*, 700.

[23] See *Ibid.*, 712–737.

[24] Ronald Goldman, *Religious Thinking from Childhood to Adolescence* (New York: The Seabury Press, 1968), 4.

[25] William James, *The Varieties of Religious Experience* (New York: New American Library, 1958), 40.

[26] *Ibid.*

[27] *Ibid.* James does not include a "religious instinct" in his list of "special human instincts" (*Principles*, 712–737).

[28] See James, *Principles*, 743–746; Richards, *Darwin*, 437.

[29] See Richards, *Darwin*, 437,n93.

[30] See *Ibid.*, 437–439.

[31] See James, *Principles*, 851–890.

[32] *Ibid.*, 851. James insisted that the "organic structure of the mind" must rather be "understood as congenital variations, 'accidental' in the first instance, but then transmitted as fixed features of the race" (*Ibid.*).

[33] James, *Varieties*,73, 389. For his part, Peirce claimed that while reason is not identical with instinct, it is rooted in the latter, and that it is by virtue of this "instinctive mind" ("faculty"/"natural disposition"/ "innate cognitive habit") that man has an affinity to and a "vague and indeterminate" certainty about God's reality as being "vaguely like a man" (see Vincent G. Potter, "'Vaguely like a Man': The Theism of Charles S. Peirce," in Robert J. Roth, ed., *God Knowable and Unknowable* [New York: Fordham University Press, 1973], 245–249, 253).

[34] James, *Varieties*, 61–63, 383–391.

[35] Wayne Proudfoot has argued that notwithstanding James' own suggestion that the religious sentiment is more like a sensation than a thought, it really does "assume certain concepts and thoughts," and therefore has the epistemic status of a "hypothesis . . . thoughts, hunches, or guesses" (W. Proudfoot, *Religious Experience* [Berkeley: University of California Press, 1985], 163; see also *Ibid.*, 160, 169).

[36] James, *Varieties*, 58–75, 383–391.

[37] McDougall, *Social Psychology*, 27.

[38] *Ibid.*

[39] *Ibid.*, 30.

[40] *Ibid.*, 33–34.

[41] *Ibid.*, 34–35; see also: Donceel, *Philosophical Anthropology*, 156.

[42] McDougall, *Social Psychology*, 35.

[43] *Ibid.*, 309.

[44] *Ibid.*, 312.

[45] *Ibid.*, 317.

[46] *Ibid.*, 59–61; and *Supra*, Chapter V.

[47] *Ibid.*, 61, 317–320.

[48] *Ibid.*, 60.

[49] *Ibid.*, 310–312.

[50] *Ibid.*, 322; also: *Ibid.*, 61, 312, 317, 327.

[51] William K. Wright, "The Genesis of the Categories," *The Journal of Philosophy, Psychology and Scientific Methods* X.24 (November 20, 1913), 653.

[52] *Ibid.*, 652–654.

[53] See Lester M. Sdorow, *Psychology* (Madison, Wisc.: Brown and Benchmark, 1993), 12–13, 429; Donceel, *Philosophical Anthropology*, 155; *NCE* 7:548.

[54] J.J. Smith, "Religious Development of Children," in *Child Psychology: Child Development and Modern Education*, ed. Charles E. Skinner and Philip L. Harriman (New York: Macmillan, 1941), 274.

[55] *Ibid.*, 276–285.

[56] *Ibid.*, 276.

[57] See J. Piaget, *The Principles of Genetic Epistemology* (London: Routledge and Kegan Paul, 1972), 10–11; *Language and Learning, The Debate Between Jean Piaget and Noam Chomsky*, ed. Massimo Piattelli-Palmarini (Cambridge: Harvard University Press, 1980), 23, 24, 241.

[58] Piaget, *Principles*, 19, 56, 91; J. Piaget, *Biology and Knowledge* (Chicago and London: University of Chicago Press, 1971), 269–271; Piattelli-Palmarini, *Language and Learning*, 30, 59, 231, 238.

[59] J. Piaget, *The Moral Judgment of the Child* (New York: The Free Press, 1965), 399; Piaget, *Principles*, 91; J. Piaget, *The Origins of Intelligence in Children* (New York: International Universities Press, 1975), 2–3. Dan Sperber, incidentally, accuses Piaget and his followers of "prejudice" against "any kind of innatist hypothesis" (see his comments in Piattelli-Palmarini, *Language and Learning*, 78–79).

[60] See L. Kohlberg, *The Philosophy of Moral Development* (San Francisco: Harper and Row, 1981), 294–307; *Moral Development, Moral Education, and Kohlberg*, ed. Brenda Munsey (Birmingham, Ala.: Religious Education Press, 1980), 130–160, 269–358; J. Fowler, *Stages of Faith* (San Francisco: Harper and Row, 1981).

[61] Pierre Bovet, *The Child's Religion* (New York: E.P. Dutton and Co., 1928), esp. 33–47; David Elkind, "The Development of Religious Understanding in Children and Adolescents," in *Research on Religious Development*, ed. Merton P. Strommen (New York: Hawthorn Books, 1971), 662.

[62] J. Piaget, *The Child's Conception of the World* (Totowa, N.J.: Rowman and Littlefield, 1983), 268, 354, 378, 381–385; Piaget, *Moral Judgment*, 371, 375, 376.

[63] See: Konrad Lorenz, "Kant's Doctrine of the A Priori in the Light of Contemporary Biology," in *General Systems*, edited by L. von Bertalanffy and A. Rapoport (Ann Arbor: Society for General Systems Research, 1962), Volume VII, 23–35; K. Lorenz, *Evolution and Modification of Behavior* (Chicago: The University of Chicago, 1967), 40–41; Richards, "The Innate and the Learned," 111–133; Richards, *Darwin*, 528–536; Sdorow, *Psychology*, 429, 715.

[64] C.G. Jung, *The Archetypes and the Collective Unconscious*, in *The Collected Works of C.G. Jung*, Volume 9, Part I, ed. William McGuire et al. (Princeton: Princeton University Press, 1959), 3.

[65] *Ibid.*, 42, 3.

[66] *Ibid.*, 42.

[67] *Ibid.*, 42, 43, 77, 156.

[68] *Ibid.*, 66, 57.

[69] *Ibid.*, 77.

[70] *Ibid.*, 66.

[71] *Ibid.*

[72] *Ibid.* See for concrete examples of various archetypes: *Ibid.*, 21ff (Shadow); *Ibid.*, 25ff (Anima); *Ibid.*, 37 (Wise Old Man); *Ibid.*, 81ff (Mother); *Ibid.*, 151ff (Child).

[73] See Verkamp, *Evolution of Religion*, 191–192 ns.156–158.

[74] See *Ibid.*, 175–176.

[75] Jung, *The Archetypes*, 66; C.G. Jung, *Man and His Symbols* (New York: Doubleday, 1964), 67.

[76] Jung, *The Archetypes*, 79, 48.

[77] *Ibid.*, 79.

[78] Jung, *Man and His Symbols*, 69.

[79] *Ibid.*, 76; Jung, *The Archetypes*, 43.

[80] Jung, *Man and His Symbols*, 79.

[81] Jung, *The Archetypes*, 79.

[82] *Ibid.*

[83] *Ibid.*, 42.

[84] *Ibid.*, 58, 66–67.

[85] *Ibid.*, 48.

[86] *Ibid.*, 162.

[87] *Ibid.*, 174.

[88] *Ibid.*, 48, 58–59, 160; Jung, *Man and His Symbols*, 75.

[89] Jung, *The Archetypes*, 79–80.

[90] *Ibid.*, 48–50.

[91] See Martin E.P. Seligman and Joanne L. Hager, *Biological Boundaries of Learning* (New York: Appleton-Century-Crofts, 1972), 1. For a good general introduction to the question, see Mary Midgley, *Beast and Man, The Roots of Human Nature* (Ithaca, NY: Cornell University Press, 1978), 51–82. Rejecting the *tabula rasa* theory of the behaviorists, Midgley concludes that "the nature of a species consists in a certain range of powers and tendencies, a repertoire, inherited and forming a fairly firm characteristic pattern, though conditions after birth may vary the details quite a lot" (*Ibid.*, 58).

[92] Charles J. Lumsden and Edward O. Wilson, *Genes, Mind, and Culture* (Cambridge, MA: Harvard University Press, 1981), 370.

[93] *Ibid.*, 43–48.

[94] *Ibid.*, 38–43.

[95] *Ibid.*, 370.

[96] *Ibid.*, 36, 95–96; see also Michael Ruse, *Taking Darwin Seriously* (Oxford: Basil Blackwell, 1986), 143.

[97] Lumsden and Wilson, *Genes*, 71–96; Ruse, *Taking Darwin Seriously*, 145–147.

[98] Lumsden and Wilson, *Genes*, 92.

[99] Michael Ruse, *The Darwinian Paradigm: Essays on its history, philosophy, and religious implications* (London and New York: Routledge, 1989), 260; Ruse, *Taking Darwin Seriously*, 143–147, 161–185, 205–206, 221–223, 230–235, 251. It should be noted that the insistence by Ruse and others upon the innateness of epigenetic rules does not preclude, but rather assumes, the likelihood, suggested earlier by Herbert Spencer (see *DPP* I;549), that even though individual human beings are now born with such propensities, the human race itself may have acquired them through experience somewhere along the line of its evolution and possibly after the first humans had already appeared.

[100] Ruse, *Taking Darwin Seriously*, 155–178.

[101] *Ibid.*, 156–161, 164–166, 168.

[102] *Ibid.*, 144–147, 169–170.

[103] *Ibid.*, 184, 178–206.

[104] *Ibid.*, 263.

[105] *Ibid.*, 263.

[106] *Ibid.*, 221.

[107] *Ibid.*

[108] *Ibid.*, 223.

[109] *Ibid.*, 230.

[110] *Ibid.*, 223, 230.

[111] E. O. Wilson, *Sociobiology: The New Synthesis* (Cambridge, Mass.: Belknap Press, 1975), 562.

[112] E. O. Wilson, *On Human Nature* (Cambridge, Mass.: Harvard University Press, 1978), 177, 188; Wilson, *Sociobiology*, 562.

[113] Wilson, *On Human Nature*, 205–209.

[114] *Ibid.*, 177.

[115] Ruse, *Taking Darwin Seriously*, 175, 176.

[116] *Ibid.*, 177–178.

[117] *Ibid.*, 175.

[118] *Ibid.*, 177.

[119] *Ibid.*

[120] *Ibid.*

[121] *Ibid.*, 195.

[122] *Ibid.*, 178.

[123] J. Z. Young, *Philosophy and the Brain* (Oxford, New York: Oxford University Press, 1987), 18–20.

[124] *Ibid.*, 190, 191–207.

[125] *Ibid.*, 190.

[126] *Ibid.*, 149–150, 204.

[127] *Ibid.*, 1–78.

[128] *Ibid.*, 79.

[129] *Ibid.*, 20–21.

[130] See *Ibid.*, 166–168. *Gestalt* psychology, it may be noted in passing, also emphasized the *active* role of the mind in organizing sensations into coherent wholes that in some way differ from the sum of their parts, and the comprehension of which somehow precedes meaningful apprehension of the parts (see Wolfgang Koehler, *The Task of Gestalt Psychology* Princeton: Princeton University Press, 1969, 9–11, 46–53; Sdorow, *Psychology*, 13–14, 197–198).

CHAPTER TWO

Spiritual Instinct/ Predisposition

The naturalistic/materialistic conclusion that the religious sense of mystery can be reduced to nothing more than a brain state has been challenged by many other past and present thinkers on the grounds that the mind is a faculty of the soul, and as such has a profound influence upon the operation of the brain. Some of these thinkers have expressed their challenge to the naturalistic/materialistic interpretation by emphasizing along Aristotelian/Kantian lines that body and soul (brain and mind) are, in the final analysis, two aspects of the one same self. In their perspective, in other words, the human soul is thought of not as a being that is complete in itself and existing for its own sake, but as a vital principle or intrinsic source from which all the faculties or powers of the knowing subject originate. To their way of thinking, therefore, any dimension of human consciousness, like the religious sense of mystery, must be explained as a product of an animated or informed brain (that is, of a brain that is "operating under the formal causality of the soul") and not of the brain as "a mere material system."[1] Several of the following chapters of this book will investigate such interpretations of the religious sense of mystery. Other of these past and present thinkers have taken a more dualistic approach in their challenge of the naturalistic/materialistic view, arguing that the body and soul consist of two separate and independent substances, and that the mind, as a faculty of the soul, is also, therefore, to some extent independent of the brain, and has a structure of its own that can and does interact or run parallel to any genetically predisposed brain.[2] One such line of dualistic thinking, which would have us conceive of the

19

religious sense of mystery as a spiritual instinct or predisposition of the soul, and which we will be examining in the remainder of this chapter, surfaced during the seventeenth and eighteenth century discussion of innate ideas by the likes of Lord Herbert of Cherbury, Descartes, and Leibniz.[3]

In his attempt to explain how divine providence, without any special revelation, had provided all humans with a rational ability to choose for themselves between the conflicting truth claims of all the various religions,[4] Lord Herbert had identified certain common notions as the product of man's natural instinct.[5] That humans have been "endowed in the primeval plan of Nature" with such an instinct,[6] he goes on to say, should hardly be surprising. For if instinct is, as we know, operative "throughout the elements, minerals, plants and animals" for the sake of their "self-preservation," "why should it not manifest itself in ourselves?"[7] When it does, he concluded, "self-preservation assumes a higher form, and appears as the impulse for salvation; it becomes a spiritual in place of a biological impulse."[8] Such an innate instinct, he continues, can be defined in the first place as the preeminent instance of the many faculties[9] whereby the human soul/mind is able to "conform" itself to the variety of objects it encounters.[10] When this potency has been actualized, or in other words, when the "conformity" has been achieved, the "instinct" may be defined as a *sensus*,[11] an "apprehension,"[12] or a "form of awareness."[13] Involved therein is the "fundamental apprehension of pure objectivity," whereby the human mind has an "indeterminate premonition" of the object's "presence" or "being" prior to any conception of its "whatness."[14] Its main content, however, are the "common notions," among which are to be counted the religious "ideas" of God's existence, the need for worship and repentance, the belief in eternal reward and punishment, and the close connection of piety with virtue.[15]

That such ideas are "innate," and not the product of experience,[16] is evidenced by the fact that they are "common," not, to be sure, in the sense that every infant comes into the world with fully fledged ideas about God, nor in the sense that they are revealed in every man "whether he will or no,"[17] but at least virtually, in the sense that they are implicit in the human mind, and can be discovered upon the attainment of maturity by any man who is not "headstrong, foolish, weak-minded and imprudent," but "normal."[18] Although such "ideas" are the product of a "spiritual" faculty, and provide humans with a share in divine "wisdom,"[19] they do not lose their affinity with "natural instinct," whose "nature" it is "to fulfill itself irrationally, that is to say without foresight."[20] The knowledge they provide is not only immediate, direct and preconceptual, it is also sometimes beyond the comprehension of human reason, and must simply be accepted as indisputable.[21] It is also instinctive in the sense that it excites in man a desire for self-preservation, or happiness, in the long run, and triggers behavior conducive to the achievement of that end, even though the nature of the latter remains "uncertain or obscure."[22]

Lord Herbert consciously linked his interpretation of the natural instinct and its manifestation in the "common notions" with what some of the later Stoic philosophers (e.g., Cicero and Epictetus) had written about the "*lumen naturae*" and its production of the *notiones innatae* (*koinai ennoiai*), which were called *anticipationes* (*prolepseis*) to the extent that they were thought of as being a type of universal, intuitive cognition that "anticipates" but nonetheless differs radically from any kind of conceptual or empirical knowledge.[23] A similarly naive version of innate knowledge was being propounded in the seventeenth century by Richard Carpenter, Edward Stillingfleet, Robert South, and other English divines.[24] And it has been argued by some commentators that even Descartes and Leibniz were inclined to conceive of the virtual innateness of ideas along such lines.[25] But an alternate, and perhaps more obvious, reading of their writings would suggest that in both Descartes and Leibniz can be seen a tendency to return to the doctrine of the earlier Stoics, according to whom ideas were thought of as being virtually innate only in the sense that the human mind has a natural predisposition to form them.[26]

To account for such a natural predisposition that can give rise to the innate ideas and propositions of not only mathematics and science, but also and especially of such ideas and propositions as lie at the heart of religion (e.g., the idea of God),[27] Descartes distinguished two types of human instincts. The one instinct, which we ("*qua* animals") share with animals, consists of a specific natural impulse to preserve our bodies and to enjoy corporeal pleasure.[28] This instinct, he says, "should not always be followed," because "blind" and easily "corrupted,"[29] it can sometimes mislead one into doing what is hurtful, "as in the case of the dropsical patient" who satisfies his thirst only to his own disadvantage.[30] The other instinct is one that "is in us *qua* human beings, and is purely intellectual: it is the natural light or 'mental vision.'[31] (*Lumiere naturelle ou 'intuitus mentis'*)."[32] "This is the only instinct," Descartes adds, "which I think one should trust."[33] Contrasting his own view with that of Lord Herbert, who had emphasized "universal consent" as the primary test of truth, and noting elsewhere that the "light of grace" may also be necessary to solicit assent to the sometimes "obscure matters of faith,"[34] Descartes claimed that as for himself, there was no other criterion of truth "except the natural light."[35] The fact that God has endowed all humans with this natural light does not mean, however, that everyone will have the same grasp of the truth. Descartes admits that "hardly anyone makes good use of that light."[36] Our bodies and minds so interact, he says, that the "liberty to think" of adults, and even more so of babes, or of people who are sick or asleep, is often overwhelmed by sensory stimuli.[37]

"Unregulated inquiries and confused reflections" can also "confound the natural light and blind our mental powers," and "those who so become accustomed to walk in darkness weaken their eye sight so much that afterwards they cannot bear the light of the day."[38] But used properly, that is, when one is "wise" enough "to distinguish rightly between what is [clearly and distinctly] perceived, and what merely seems or appears to be clear and distinct,"[39] this "faculty"[40] of knowledge which God has given us can never disclose to us any object which is not true . . . in as much as it apprehends it clearly and distinctly," unless, of course, we are to suppose, unreasonably, that God is a "deceiver."[41] That "perception"[42] is "clear," Descartes notes, "which is present and apparent to an attentive mind, in the same way as we assert that we see objects clearly when, being present to the regarding eye, they operate upon it with sufficient strength."[43] The perception is "distinct" when it is "so precise and different from all other objects [perceptions] that it contains within itself nothing but what is clear."[44]

Descartes will also sometimes refer to a perception that is clear and distinct as an "intuition," and understand the latter, therefore, as "not the fluctuating testimony of the senses, nor the misleading judgment that proceeds form the floundering constructions of imagination, but the conception which an unclouded and attentive mind gives us so readily and distinctly that we are wholly freed from doubt about that which we understand."[45] Relying as it does on "immediately presented evidence," it is far less discursive than "deductive" thought, and in many ways, despite profound differences between the two thinkers, bears a close resemblance to the kind of "instinctive, spontaneous, immediate, and direct apprehension of the truth" that his contemporary, Blaise Pascal, had in mind when he talked about "the heart" to describe what he considered to be man's emotive-cognition of the first principles.[46] Like

Augustine, Plotinus,[47] and many other past and contemporaneous thinkers,[48] Descartes, as we have seen, described such "intuitive knowledge" also as "an elucidation of the mind, by which it sees things in the light of God, which it pleases him to show it, by a direct impression of the divine light upon our understanding, which in this case is not considered as an agent, but solely as receiving the rays of divinity."[49] When Thomas Hobbes objected that such talk of "mental illumination" was too "metaphorical," and therefore, of little "argumentative" value, Descartes replied that "as no one can be unaware . . . by mental illumination is meant clearness of cognition."[50]

But can we, according to Descartes, really enjoy such a direct and immediate, "instinctive" or "intuitive" knowledge of God and other religious "ideas"? In some passages of his writings, Descartes would seem to imply that our idea of God is innate only in the sense that by reflection upon our own imperfection, lack, and aspiration toward perfection, we can deduce the notion of a being more perfect than ourselves.[51] But in the same meditation he will insist that "in some way I have in me the notion of the infinite earlier than the finite—to wit, the notion of God before that of myself. For how would it be possible that I should know that I doubt and desire, that is to say, that something is lacking to me, and that I am not quite perfect, unless I had within me some idea of a being more perfect than myself, in comparison with which I should recognize the deficiencies of my nature?"[52] And since, according to Descartes, the idea of God necessarily implies the existence of God,[53] we know directly, immediately, "instinctively" or "intuitively," *that* God (i.e., "a substance that is infinite [eternal, immutable], independent, all-knowing, all-powerful, and [creative]")[54] exists.[55] But just as "one can certainly touch a mountain, even though he cannot embrace it," so, Descartes writes to several friends, it is one thing to "perceive" God, and quite another to "comprehend God, who is infinite."[56]

That the idea of God is the "most true, most clear, and most distinct of all the ideas that are in my mind" does not preclude the fact, Descartes admits, that "I do not comprehend the infinite," or that "in God there is an infinitude of things which I cannot comprehend, nor possibly ever reach in any way by thought."[57] For "it is of the nature of the infinite that my nature, which is finite and limited, should not understand . . . the infinitude of properties [that are] in God formally or eminently."[58] In contrast to the "mathematical truths," the "greatness of God," Descartes tells Mersenne, "is something which we cannot grasp

even though we know it."[59] "I know that God is the author of everything
. . ." he adds in a subsequent letter to Mersenne, "I say that I know this,
not that I conceive it or grasp it; because it is possible to know that God
is infinite and all powerful although our soul, being finite, cannot grasp
or conceive him . . . or put our arms around [him] as we could put them
around a tree or something else not too large for them."[60] Our
knowledge of God's existence will always remain "inadequate," and in
that sense at least God is "unthinkable."[61]

While, therefore, it may be true "that one result of Cartesian science
should be the reduction of wonder at natural phenomena,"[62] or that
"mystery is excluded by Descartes' doctrine of clear and distinct
perception, since this implies that anyone who understands a thing at all
understands it wholly,"[63] it is also true that so far as our knowledge of
God and other religious truths are concerned, Descartes would no doubt
have agreed with Blaise Pascal's conviction that "reason's last step is
the recognition that there are an infinite number of things which are
beyond it,"[64] and would have recommended "wonder" in at least the
realm that lies beyond physics.[65] For however clear and distinct may be
our knowledge *that* God exists, the nature of God will forever seem to
our finite human minds something "rare and extraordinary," or, in other
words, an object of wonder.[66]

Although Leibniz did not follow Descartes in distinguishing
explicitly between two types of human instinct, he did, for all practical
purposes, differentiate the same two types of knowledge Descartes had
had in mind, namely, an "instinctive" knowledge of the kind that we
share with animals, and secondly, a "natural light" that is unique to man
as a rational creature. By "instinct," Leibniz wrote, "everyone understands . . . an inclination which an animal has—with no conception of
the reason for it—towards something which is suitable to it."[67]
"Instincts" also occur in humans, he continued, and even though "our
artificial way of life has almost wiped out most of them," we "ought to
pay more attention" to them.[68] Among such instincts are to be counted
those that incline humans to employ "the laws of inference" (e.g., the
principle of contradiction),[69] others—the "instincts of conscience"—that
lead "straight away and without reasoning, to part of what reason
commands" (e.g., "to pursue joy and flee sorrow,"[70] to feel compassion
for our own kind, to loathe incest, etc.),[71] and still others of a religious
sort, like the "natural feeling that has brought about the *tradition* that
there is a God."[72] These instincts "do not irresistibly impel us to act,"
Leibniz admitted, because "our passions lead us to resist them, our

prejudices obscure them, and contrary customs distort them."[73] While, therefore, the knowledge they deliver is a "species" of "innate truth," it is "very often a confused one,"[74] or, a knowledge, in other words, where there is no comprehension of its logical "necessity"[75] or rationality.

The other species of innate truth according to Leibniz is that yielded by the "natural light."[76] "Since the senses and induction can never teach us truths that are fully universal or absolutely necessary, but only what is and what is found in particular examples, and since we nonetheless know the universal and necessary truths of the sciences," Leibniz wrote in this letter to the Queen of Prussia, "it follows that we have drawn these truths in part from what is within us."[77] We can do this, Leibniz claimed, because "there is a light which is born within us."[78] In contrast to the "confused" knowledge delivered by the "instinctive" discovery of innate truth, this process of "illumination," as Leibniz sometimes refers to the operation of the "natural light,"[79] "contains only what is distinctly knowable,"[80] or "in a luminous way"[81] (i.e., "through ideas[82] [or] reason").[83] The way it works, according to Leibniz, is for the mind to reflect upon its own nature and thereby discover ideas that are virtually innate to it.[84] The fact that such implicit truths may be tacit and unused does not mean that the mind merely has a faculty for knowing them.[85] For, "it is known," Leibniz argued, "that for a faculty to be brought to bear upon an object there must often be not merely the faculty and the object, but also some disposition in the faculty or in the object, or in both."[86] And so, in addition to having a faculty for finding implicit truths in itself, the mind also has "a disposition, if it is thinking about them properly, to accept them."[87] Far from being a *tabula rasa*, therefore, the human mind is rather "a disposition, an aptitude, a preformation, which determines our soul and which makes it possible for [such truths] to be derived from it."[88] Just as a block of marble might be other than "wholly indifferent" to the figure of Hercules which a sculptor eventually discovers in its veins,[89] so the human mind, Leibniz concluded, enjoys a "special affinity . . . with [these truths] which makes the exercise of the faculty easy and natural [in respect to them], and which makes us call them innate."[90] Among many such ideas (like those we have of being, substance, causality, etc.),[91] is the "idea of God," which the mind has a special propensity to fashion, not merely out of the perceived relation between certain ideas derived form sense experience,[92] but from within, by reflection upon itself.[93]

As noted earlier, Leibniz was of the view that the "natural light" contained "only what is distinctly knowable."[94] It should be noted, however, that according to Leibniz there are certain things, such as the union of the divine and human natures in Christ, whose existence might be grasped by the "natural light" enhanced by faith, but whose nature, although not contrary to reason, remains nonetheless "above reason," or beyond human comprehension, so any "idea" of them can only be described as an "idea of mystery."[95]

Most modern thinkers have not been so dualistic in their conception of the relation of the body and soul as were the likes of Lord Herbert, Descartes, and Leibniz. Among the few who have been, the most noteworthy in recent times have been John Eccles and Richard Swinburne. Neither examines in any great detail the exact nature of any "spiritual instinct." But both seem to argue for its existence and its causal influence upon the operation of the human brain. While Eccles devoted most of his work to explaining how "hominid evolution was uniquely dependent on the primate ancestry providing a superbly developed nervous system,"[96] he insisted that only a "mysterious . . . and supernatural spiritual creation" can explain the origin of "souls,"[97] which not only facilitate "propositional speech, abstract thought, and self-consciousness,"[98] but also, like the software of a computer,[99] program the brain "to wonder," as his fellow scientist Werner Heisenberg put it, at "the central order of things,"[100] or, in the words of Hinshelwood, to seek "instinctively" for "something personal behind the processes of nature," or for what traditionally has been called the "vision of God."[101]

For his part, Swinburne argues that while the human soul can be said to have its roots in the animal soul,[102] he also insists that medieval thinkers were right in ascribing to humans a rational or intellectual soul, or, in other words, a "special kind of soul, with "mental capacities which went beyond those of animals."[103] "What seems to have happened in the course of evolution," Swinburne writes, is that when genetic changes gave to animals beliefs and desires, they were beliefs about how to attain fairly immediate goals and desires for those goals.[104] But then something new happened. The soul passed from being passive to being active and "structured by causally influential beliefs and desires" of a more "sophisticated sort."[105] "Gradually our ancestors began to have more sophisticated beliefs and desires which came to form a structure, so that the causal efficacy of beliefs and desires now included causing other beliefs and desires."[106] This gave the organism the "ability to plan" and the "purpose to pursue plans over a continued period of time."[107] The human soul, in other words, is "not totally soft"[108] or "passive and structureless";[109] it is rather "structured and active";[110] "it has to it some structure so that its shape in some parts is determined by its shape in other parts, and its shape to some extent determines that of the brain."[111] Part and parcel of that structure from the very beginning has been "a capacity for reaching out to a God in the world to come," a capacity for "mythologizing" about the "origin and destiny of the world and of man within it."[112]

NOTES

[1] See Donceel, *Philosophical Anthropology*, 177.

[2] See, for example, Rene Descartes, *Discourse on Method* IV, GB 31: 51–52.

[3] For a more direct discussion of various theories about the actual or virtual innateness of ideas, see Verkamp, *Evolution of Religion*, 159–168.

[4] See J. Samuel Preus, *Explaining Religion* (New Haven and London: Yale University Press, 1987), 23–39.

[5] Lord Herbert of Cherbury, *De Veritate*, translated with an Introduction by Meyrick H. Carre (Bristol: J. W. Arrowsmith, Ltd., 1937), 115–145.

[6] *Ibid.*, 121.

[7] *Ibid.*, 119, 123, 136.

[8] *Ibid.*, 31, 139, 142–143.

[9] See Descartes' comment on Lord Herbert's use of this term: *Infra*, n.40.

[10] Lord Herbert, *De Veritate*, 122–123.

[11] *Ibid.*, 153, 19.

[12] *Ibid.*, 122.

[13] *Ibid.*, 33.

[14] *Ibid.*, 40, 208.

[15] *Ibid.*, 29, 31, 33, 293, 296, 298, 300.

[16] *Ibid.*, 132.

[17] *Ibid.*, 125–127, 38.

[18] *Ibid.*, 122, 125, 126.

[19] *Ibid.*, 126.

[20] *Ibid.*, 120.

[21] *Ibid.*, 120–121, 125, 140.

[22] *Ibid.*, 126, 132, 135–137, 139, 142–145.

[23] *Ibid.*, 125–126, 42, n2. See also Cicero, *Tusculan-Disputations* (London: W. Heinemann, 1927), I.XIII, 35–37; Cicero, "On the Law," I.8, 24, in *Selected Works of Cicero* (New York: The Classics Club, 1948), 229–232; *The Discourses of Epictetus*, GB 12: 106, 127, 150, 182; Diogenes Laertius, *Lives of Eminent Philosophers* (London: W. Heinemann, 1965), 153, 161, 163; R. G. Kottich, *Die Lehre von den angeborenen Ideen seit Herbert von Cherbury* (Berlin: Verlagsbuchhandlung von Richard Schoetz, 1917), 7–13, 16–22; F. Copleston, *A History of Philosophy*, Volume 1, *Greece and Rome,* Part II (Garden City, NY: Doubleday and Company, Inc., 1962), 131, 163, 176.

[24] See John W. Yolton, *John Locke and the Way of Ideas* (Oxford: Oxford University Press, 1956), 31, 37–40.

[25] In his "Letter to Hyperaspistes, August 1641," Descartes stated that the infant "nonetheless has in itself the ideas of God, of itself and of all such truths as are called self-evident, in the same way as adult human beings have these ideas when they are not attending to them; for it does not acquire these ideas later on, as it grows older." *The Philosophical Writings of Descartes*, Volume III, *Correspondence*, translated by John Cottingham, Robert Stoothoff, Dugald Murdoch, Anthony Kenny (Cambridge: Cambridge University Press, 1984), 190. See also David E. Cooper, "Innateness: Old and New," *The Philosophical Review* LXXXI (October, 1972), 468–469; C.D. Broad, *Leibniz, An Introduction* (London: Cambridge University Press, 1975), 138–139.

[26] In his *Notes Against a Programme*, Descartes disclaimed ever having argued that ideas are innate in any other than a dispositional manner. *The Philosophical Works of Descartes*, trans. by E. Haldane and G. R. T. Ross (Cambridge: Cambridge University Press, 1983), 442; G. W. Leibniz, *New Essays Concerning Human Understanding* (New York: Macmillan, 1896), 46, 76, 84, 85, 105; Verkamp, *Evolution of Religion*, 166–168.

[27] See especially: Descartes, *Meditations* III, *GB* 31: 86–89; IV, *GB* 31: 89; V, *GB* 31: 93–94; *Reply to Second Objections*, *GB* 31:120; "Letter to Hyperaspistes, August 1641," 190; *Principles of Philosophy*, Part I, LIV, Haldane, *Works*, 241; *The Search After Truth*, Haldane, *Works*, 310; *Notes Against a Programme*, Haldane, *Works*, 448.

[28] "Letter to Mersenne, October 16, 1639," Cottingham, *Correspondence*, 140.

[29] *The Search After Truth*, Haldane, *Works*, 312.

[30] *Meditations* III, *GB* 31: 83; Reply to Second Objections, *GB* 31:124.

[31] "Letter to Mersenne, October 16, 1639," 140; *Meditations* III, *GB* 31:83.

[32] See *Oeuvres de Descartes*, ed. Charles Adam and Paul Tannery (Paris: Librairie Philosophique J. Vrin, 1969), II: 599.

[33] "Letter to Mersenne, October 16, 1639," 140.

[34] *Reply to Second Objections*, *GB* 31:125. In *Rules for Direction*, Descartes notes that belief in the "obscure matters of faith" is an action, "not of our intelligence, but of our will" (*GB* 31:4).

[35] "Letter to Mersenne, October 16, 1639," 139; see also: *Discourse on Method* III, *GB* 31:50; *Reply to Sixth Objections*, *GB* 31:224.

[36] "Letter to Mersenne, October 16, 1639," 139.

[37] "Letter to Hyperaspistes, August 1641," 189–190; "Conversation with Burman, 16 April 1648," Cottingham, *Correspondence*, 336.

[38] *Rules for Direction*, *GB* 31:5.

[39] *Reply to Seventh Objections*, *GB* 31:238. In the *Meditations* Descartes states that "all things which I perceive very clearly and distinctly are true" (*Meditations* III, *GB* 31:82).

[40] Note that although Descartes criticizes Lord Herbert for having needlessly multiplied "faculties" and leading people into thinking of faculties as "little entities in our soul" ("Letter to Mersenne, October 16, 1639," 139–140), he does himself often refer to the "natural light" as a "faculty" in the sense of a "potentiality" (see *Notes Against a Programme*, 444).

[41] *Principles of Philosophy* I: XXX, 231.

[42] Descartes, "in contrast to modern usage, reserves the verb 'to perceive' (Latin: *percipere*) for the purely mental apprehension of the intellect" (John Cottingham, *A Descartes Dictionary* [Oxford: Blackwell Publishers, 1993], 143).

[43] *Principles of Philosophy* I:XLV, 237; *Reply to Second Objections*, *GB* 31:124–125.

[44] *Principles of Philosophy* I:XLV, 237.

[45] *Rules for Direction* III, *GB* 31:4.

[46] *Ibid.*; *Reply to Sixth Objections*, *GB* 31:224. Blaise Pascal, *Pensees and Other Writings* (Oxford: Oxford University Press, 1995), 35–36, 58, 157–158; see also Copleston, *History*, volume 4, *Modern Philosophy: Descartes to Leibniz*, 171–173.

[47] See Verkamp, *Evolution of Religion*, 185,ns.70 and 71; Cottingham, *Dictionary*, 32–33, 94.

[48] Many seventeenth century thinkers, such as Henry More, Nathaniel Culverwel, Walter Charleton, Robert Ferguson, and Ralph Cudworth, all spoke of the "active sagacity," the "intellectual lamp," the "Power," the "natural Sagacity," or the "innate vigour and activity of the mind itself," whereby the idea of the Deity and other "virtually innate" ideas are produced upon the occasion of external stimuli (see Yolton, *Locke,* 40, 41, 43, 58).

[49] "Letter to Newcastle, March or April, 1648" (*Descartes Dictionary*, translated and edited by John M. Morris [New York: Philosophical Library, 1971], 102).

[50] *Reply to Third Objections*, *GB* 31:141.

[51] See *Meditations* III, *GB* 31:88; Copleston, *History* 4:112–113.

[52] See *Meditations* III, *GB* 31:86.

[53] *Meditations* IV, *GB* 31:89.

[54] *Meditations* III, *GB* 31:86.

[55] *Meditations* IV, *GB* 31:89.

[56] "Letter to Mersenne, 27 May, 1630," *Correspondence*, 25; "Letter to Clerselier," Morris, *Dictionary*, 32.

[57] *Meditations* III, *GB* 31:86.

[58] *Ibid.*

[59] "Letter to Mersenne, 15 April, 1630," *Correspondence*, 23.

[60] *Ibid.*, 25; *Reply to Second Objections*, *GB* 31:112.

[61] *Reply to Second Objections*, *GB* 31: 123, 127; *Principles of Philosophy* VI, 241.

[62] Descartes, *Passions of the Soul*, 61,n17. Defining wonder as "a sudden surprise of the soul which makes it tend to consider attentively those objects which seem to it rare and extraordinary" (*Passions of the Soul*, Art. 70, p. 56; Art. 53, p. 52; Art. 75, p. 59), Descartes wrote that wonder "disposes us to the acquisition of the sciences," but that "we should still try afterwards to emancipate ourselves from it as much as possible" (*Ibid.*, Art. 76, pp. 60–61). An "excess of wonder," he added, "prolongs the sickness of the blindly curious—that is those who investigate rarities only to wonder at them and not to understand them" (*Ibid.*, Art. 78, p. 61). In *The Search After Truth*, Descartes has Eudorus disclaim any such curiosity (Haldane, *Works*, 307–309).

[63] Michael B. Foster, *Mystery and Philosophy* (London: SCM Press LTD, 1957), 22,n3, 53; Bernard J. Verkamp, *The Senses of Mystery* (Scranton: University of Scranton Press, 1997), 2–3.

[64] Pascal, *Pensees*, 62.

[65] See Descartes, *Passions of the Soul*, 61,n17.

[66] *Ibid.*, Art. 70, p.56.

[67] G. W. Leibniz, *New Essays on Human Understanding*, translated and edited by Peter Remnant and Jonathan Bennett (Cambridge: Cambridge University Press, 1996), Book III, xi, 8:351; I, ii, 3:90.

[68] *Ibid.*, III, xi, 8:351.

[69] *Ibid.*, I, ii, 4:91.

[70] *Ibid.*, I, ii, 9:93.

[71] *Ibid.*

[72] *Ibid.*

[73] *Ibid.*

[74] *Ibid.*, I, ii, 9:94; I, ii, 4:91; I, i, 21:84. It should be noted that according to Leibniz, ideas (or knowledge) can be "obscure or clear"; it is "obscure" if it "does not suffice for recognizing the thing represented, as when I merely remember some flower or animal which I have once seen but not well enough to recognize it when it is placed before me and to distinguish it from similar ones." *Meditations on Knowledge, Truth, and Ideas*, in G. W. Leibniz, *Philosophical Papers and Letters*, translated and edited, with an introduction by Leroy E. Loemker Chicago: The University of Chicago Press, 1956, 448; it is "clear" when "it makes it possible for me to recognize the thing represented" (*Ibid.*, 449). "Clear" knowledge can in turn be "confused" or "distinct"; it is "confused" when "I cannot enumerate one by one the marks which are sufficient to distinguish the thing from others," as, for example, when I recognize something as being "red" but "cannot explain to a blind man what red is," and can explain such a quality to others only "by bringing them into the presence of the thing and making them see" (*Ibid.*, 449); it is "distinct" when we can "distinguish something [e.g., gold] from all other bodies by sufficient marks" (*Ibid.*). A "distinct" idea, in turn, can be either "inadequate" or "adequate" to the extent that every ingredient that enters into a distinct idea is or is not itself "known distinctly" (*Ibid.*, 450). Leibniz also adds a distinction between knowledge that is "blind and symbolic" and knowledge that is "intuitive," the former referring to the kind of knowledge we have of, say a polygon, without any real grasp of the meaning of its "thousand different sides," the latter to the kind of knowledge we have when we have a "simultaneous" appreciation of "all the concepts" composing a complex idea (*Ibid.*, 450). Leibniz draws these distinctions in a number of his works (see also, for example, the *New Essays*, II, xxix, 2–16: 255–263). It should also be noted that in the *Discourse on Metaphysics*, Leibniz distinguishes between "ideas," as "expressions which are in the soul, whether conceived or not," and "notions or concepts," as those expressions in the soul "which are conceived or formed" (*Philosophical Papers and Letters*, 494).

[75] *Ibid.*, I, ii, 4–11. For further discussion, see Robert McRae, *Leibniz: Perception, Apperception, and Thought* (Toronto and Buffalo: University of Toronto Press, 1976), 120–125.

[76] Leibniz, *New Essays*, I, ii, 9:94.

[77] As cited in McRae, *Leibniz*, 117.

[78] *Ibid.*

[79] Leibniz, *New Essays*, I, ii, 4:91.

[80] *Ibid.*, I, ii, 9:94; I, i, 21:84. See also, *Supra*, note 74.

[81] *Ibid.*, I, ii, 1:89.

[82] *Ibid.*, I, ii, 4:91.

[83] *Ibid.*, I, ii, 2:89.

[84] *Ibid.*, I, i, 21:84.

[85] *Ibid.*, I, i, 5:79; I, i, 21:84.

[86] *Ibid.*, I, i, 5:79.

[87] *Ibid.*, I, i, 21:84.

[88] *Ibid.*, Preface, 52; Book I, i, 11:80.

[89] *Ibid.*, Preface, 52; Book I, i, 27:87.

[90] *Ibid.*, I, i, 11:80.

[91] *Ibid.*, I, iii, 18:105.

[92] See Copleston, *Descartes to Leibniz*, 323.

[93] Leibniz, *New Essays*, I, i, 1–5; 74–76; I, ii, 122:96; I, iii, 15:105.

[94] *Ibid.*, I, ii, 9:94; I, i, 21:84.

[95] See the discussion of comments made by Leibniz in this regard in his letters to Tournemine and De Posses, in Robert Merrihew Adams, *Leibniz, Determinist, Theist, Idealist* (New York and Oxford: Oxford University Press, 1994), 303–305, 296.

[96] John C. Eccles, *Evolution of the Brain: Creation of the Self* (London and New York: Routledge, 1989), 217.

[97] See *Ibid.*, 23–37; also: J. C. Eccles, "Cultural Evolution versus Biological Evolution," *Zygon*, volume 8, 3–4 (1973): 289, 292; John C. Eccles, *The Human Psyche* (Berlin: Springer International, 1980), 235–237.

[98] Eccles, "Cultural Evolution," 292.

[99] Eccles, *Evolution of the Brain*, 238; J. C. Eccles, *The Human Mystery* (Berlin, Heidelberg, New York: Springer International, 1979), 98–122.

[100] Eccles, *The Human Psyche*, 244–45.

[101] *Ibid.*, 245.

[102] Richard Swinburne, *The Evolution of the Soul* (Oxford: Clarendon Press, 1986), 181–182, 193, 195.

[103] *Ibid.*, 183. Swinburne, it may be noted, shares Eccles' conviction that some kind of "special creation" must be posited to account for the existence of the human consciousness (see *Ibid.*, 198–199; also: Richard Swinburne, *The Existence of God* [Oxford: Clarendon Press, 1989], 152–179).

[104] Swinburne, *Evolution of the Soul*, 296.

[105] *Ibid.*, 297.

[106] *Ibid.*, 296–297.

[107] *Ibid.*, 297.

[108] *Ibid.*, 291.

[109] *Ibid.*, 297.

[110] *Ibid.*

[111] *Ibid.*, 291.

[112] *Ibid.*, 211.

CHAPTER THREE

Emotive/Intuitive Disposition

Consistent with Aristotle's conception of the soul as the active principle of all life processes, Immanuel Kant came to view the mind not as some separate substance, but as one aspect of the human self by which the data of sense experience is organized.[1] The mind achieves this function through a process of forming judgments. By judgment in general, Kant understood the faculty or capacity of the knowing subject to either determinantly or reflectively subsume particulars under concepts or universal rules.[2] Such judgment will be of a logical sort when by ascribing certain properties to a particular object we are able to subsume it under a certain concept or see it as an instance of one or another universal rule (e.g., "The table is round").[3] In *The Critique of Pure Reason*, Kant listed, along with the perceptual categories of time and space, twelve categories corresponding to the various forms of logical judgment.[4] Since Kant considered it the function of the categories of theoretical knowledge to synthesize the data of sense intuition, he did not consider them applicable to realities such as God, the soul, the cosmos, freedom, etc., which are not, and cannot be, given in sense experience.[5] He admitted that pure reason has a natural tendency to come up with such supersensible, transcendental ideas (i.e., God, the soul, etc.) as it seeks out the unconditioned unifying principles of thought and reality.[6] But, being inapplicable to the data of sense intuition, and lacking any purely intellectual intuition by which to be supplied with corresponding objects, such transcendental ideas, he said, are merely regulative[7]—i.e., stimulating further scientific research by highlighting the limits of our present concepts, but in no way constituting knowable objects (i.e., phenomena).[8] They cannot, therefore, serve as the *a priori* elements, or the categories of religious experience. And if, therefore, there is an *a priori* element in religion, it can only be found, Kant himself would seem to have concluded, along the lines of the categorical imperative of duty, which he identified in *The Critique of Practical Reason* as the *a priori* condition of our practical knowledge of good and evil.[9]

In what Kant wrote in some of his later writings, however, and especially in his *Critique of Judgement*, about the nature of aesthetic judgment, other philosophers and theologians, such as Friedrich Schleiermacher, Jakob Fries, Ernst Troeltsch, and Rudolf Otto, have found a basis for concluding that there is indeed a faculty of the human mind whereby man has the capacity to divine the mysterious dimensions of reality.[10] In referring to such a structure of the mind as a faculty, these thinkers did not have in mind to suggest that all human beings always and everywhere actually sense the mystery of reality. Otto, for example, explicitly states that neither man in general, nor "the undifferentiated aggregate of homogenous individuals," can be said to possess the faculty of divination in actuality.[11] Only "divinatory natures, particular gifted individuals" have it, he says, "in actuality."[12] It was called a faculty to imply rather that even if, by choice or because of the circumstances of their lives, not every individual develops an eye or ear for the mystery of reality, they nonetheless retain an innate predisposition toward doing so.

When such a faculty was conceived of as having been actualized, it was often described by these thinkers as consisting of a feeling. Schleiermacher, for example, true to his earlier association with the Pietistic Herrnhut fraternity, whose founder, Ludwig von Zinzendorf, had already in 1745 linked the *sensus numinis* up with the "feeling of the supernatural,"[13] had defined the actualized religious sense as a "feeling of the infinite," or the "feeling of absolute dependence."[14] Agreeing with Schleiermacher's emphasis upon the emotional side of religion,[15] but under a stronger influence from Kant's distinction of the faculty of aesthetic judgment based upon feeling from that of understanding,[16] another student of the Moravian Brotherhood, Jakob Fries, developed a doctrine of *Ahndung,* according to which the religious sense consists of an aesthetic feeling for the "mysterious presence of the Infinite in the Finite, the Eternal in the Temporal."[17] And it was the writing of Fries especially that inclined Rudolf Otto to play up the non-rational side of religion by often identifying the *sensus numinis* as simply "the numinous feeling" (*das numinose Gefuehl*).[18] To appreciate, however, what they meant thereby, it will be necessary first to take notice of Kant's interpretation of the Platonic theory of *anamnesis* (recollection).

Some earlier thinkers, including perhaps even Leibniz, had interpreted Plato's theory of recollection to mean that humans are born with actual knowledge prior to and independent of experience.[19] But, as Alfred E. Taylor has pointed out, Plato probably had in mind only to suggest that for the human soul to gain true knowledge it must first recall, or be reminded of, what it saw (the eternal, immaterial, unchangeable forms) in its state of preexistence.[20] This can and does occur only by way of sense experience. Our sense perceptions remind us of ideal standards, which none of the objects of our experience actually exhibit in and of themselves.[21] Thus, just as a coat may remind us of its owner, or a portrait of the person represented, so, according to Plato, the sight of equal sticks may remind us of equality, or the experience of a sunset, kindness, or love, might remind us of goodness and beauty.[22] The idea such reminiscence brings to mind will be obscure[23] and ultimately beyond linguistic expression.[24] But, as such, it will constitute the point from which and to which the "prolonged effort of steady thinking" must depart and return so as to "recover" the "truth" that has been lost.[25]

According to Otto, this theory of *anamnesis* was "stated in Kant with great precision," and laid the foundation for his critique of aesthetic judgment, which would in turn influence the so-called "*Ahndung* doctrine" of Schleiermacher, Fries, Goethe, and Otto himself.[26] In contrast to logical judgments, which, as we have seen, are always, according to Kant, objective, and are made with a view toward understanding,[27] aesthetic judgments are said by Kant to attribute no property to the object experienced. They are subjective, in the sense that instead of ascribing some property to the object, they simply assert something about the pleasure or pain which we feel when we represent the object to ourselves.[28] If we say that a table is beautiful, we are merely stating that "we take pleasure in it," or more accurately, that the "form of the object" conforms in a non-conceptual way with the *a priori*, heuristic, non-constitutive principle or rule of all judgments, namely, that "Nature is an intelligible unity," and, as such, enjoys a certain "finality and purposiveness."[29] We have no conception of either the rule itself or of how the particular object embodies the totality of Nature, but we *feel* that there "is some principle of order implicit in the manifold of [sensible] intuitions given to us."[30] The "idea" we have of the table's beauty is called by Kant an aesthetic idea to distinguish it from a rational idea[31] All ideas, according to Kant, are "representations referred to an object according to a certain principle, in so far as they can still never become a cognition of it."[32] Rational ideas (e.g, the ideas of God, soul, freedom, etc.) can never become a cognition, because they "involve a concept for which a commensurate intuition can never be given."[33] An aesthetic idea, on the other hand, "cannot become a cognition, because it is an intuition (of the imagination) for which an adequate concept can never be found."[34] It is the latter, namely, the aesthetic ideas, which Kant refers to as "inexponible representations," because the idea of the "totality of nature" which they connote always remains dim and obscure, and beyond any further exposition.[35] While in a rational idea, "we think more than our imagination can exhibit," in an aesthetic idea "we imagine more than our faculty of thought can explain."[36] There is a "sense of meaning," an "awareness or con-sciousness of finality," in the latter, and we *feel* a certain harmony between the various faculties of the mind (imagination, understanding, and reason), but "there is no conceptual representation of what is meant," "no concept of an end which is achieved."[37]

What Kant said in this regard, Otto suggests, is similar to what Schleiermacher strove to express in his vague discussion of the intuitions and feelings (*Anschauungen* and *Gefuehle*) experienced by human beings when, "in a spirit of absorbed submission," they con-template the "vast, living totality and reality of things as it is in nature and history," and sense something of the "sheer overplus" of reality.[38] He was trying, in other words, to distinguish piety or religion from metaphysics and ethics, by suggesting that while the latter two involve our theoretic and practical relation to the *universum*, the former affords us an "experience of this world in its profundity, the realization of its eternal content by the feeling of a contemplative and devout mind . . . the immediate apprisal of the universe as the one and the whole, transcending the mere parts which science may grasp, and at the same time the profound spiritual experience of its underlying ideal essence."[39] For Schleiermacher, Otto concludes, the relation of a genuinely religious man to the universe is like that of a man who enters a lofty Gothic cathedral, and disregarding any theoretical or practical calculations, sits quietly in a corner, and in a contemplative mood, allows himself to be "seized of its essential idea," the "real inner meaning and nature of the building."[40] "In that great cathedral which we call the universe," such a man "will become aware of the eternal ideas, the secret divine plan governing the world, and the course of events. To him the world will become, so to speak, transparent; the eternal will shine through the temporal, the infinite, which neither space nor time can comprehend, will be revealed in the finite forms of time and space."[41] Although the "groping formulation" of such "limited and inadequate" intuitions "cannot be employed as 'statements of doctrine' in the strict sense," they "are nonetheless indisputably *true*" according to Schleiermacher, and deserve to be called "*cognitions*, modes of knowing."[42]

Otto rightly credits Goethe also with having captured the cognitive nature of the feeling involved in the religious experience of the numinosity of natural phenomena.[43] Against the tendency of rationalistic -empiricism to reduce nature to a machine[44] and to see "in abstract reasoning the key to all of nature's mysteries,"[45] Goethe insisted that nature is more "organic" than it is mechanical,[46] and that its mysterious "essential forms" (*Urphaenomen*) and "divine life" can be discerned only through a "delicate . . . deep, calm contemplation"[47] that defies conceptualization, and in which "feeling is everything."[48] As Otto notes, however, the feeling that Goethe has in mind here is something other than a subjective mood that might dispose the religious person to "fantasizing and dreaming of unreal worlds."[49] Goethe was not, in other words, trying to draw an absolute contrast between feeling and knowing.[50] It was only to a certain type of knowing, namely, "reflective-dialectical knowing in the form of the concept, the definition, of logical analysis and theorizing, etc.," that the contrast was being drawn.[51] While emphasizing, therefore, the difference of the religious feeling from any kind of abstract, analytical thinking, he nonetheless clearly identified it as a "*cognitive* feeling" or a "way of knowing." In contrast to the discursive nature of logical thinking, such a cognitive feeling is "intuitive," "immediate, primordial, and original," not unlike the "simple vision" of the child.[52]

Underlying Goethe's comments in this connection was the distinction drawn by Kant between understanding (*Verstand*) and reason (*Vernunft*).[53] Reversing a similar distinction drawn earlier by some medieval thinkers and the sixteenth century German mystic, Jakob Boehme,[54] Kant attributed to understanding the power to categorize the data of experience for utilitarian purposes, while ascribing the unifying power of the transcendental ideas to reason.[55] Along with Goethe, and to some extent under his influence, nineteenth century Romantic poets, such as Samuel Taylor Coleridge, William Wordsworth, and Percy

Bysshe Shelley, and transcendentalist philosophers, such as Henry David Thoreau and Ralph Waldo Emerson, would use the afore-mentioned Kantian distinction to differentiate the abstract, atomistic "understanding" prevalent in the sciences[56] from what they called the "inner eye," the "intuition,"[57] the "Secondary Imagination,"[58] the idea-tional "energy,"[59] whereby the mind discovers its own morphological structure in the essential forms of nature,[60] and sees the world holistically as a living,[61] purposeful,[62] "metamorphically"[63] and continuously[64] evolving organism,[65] all of whose complex parts are interconnected and harmonized in the polarity of their opposition.[66] "Reason," in their view, does not "go behind" the phenomena in search of some abstract law that might explain reality or reduce it to its simplest components;[67] it rather discerns the idea working dynamically in and through the myriad forms of the phenomenal world, and sees in them the truth they symbolize.[68] What "reason" does then, in their view, is to fuse the ideal and the empirical,[69] giving rise to a "spiritualized" science, in which the lust for objectivity is sublated through the marriage of the knowing subject and the object of experience into the joy of communion with nature.[70] If this is empiricism, it is, as Goethe would say, a "delicate empiricism," because while it investigates "that which can be investigated," it "quietly revere[s] that which cannot be investigated."[71] If it is rationalism, it is, as Goethe again would say, a visual or contemplative reasoning (*anschauende Urteilskraft*) that waits for the object of experience to reveal itself to the knowing participant in its nature.[72]

It was in the "*Ahndung* doctrine" of Jakob Fries, however, that Otto thought the Platonic notion of *anamnesis* and the Kantian critique of aesthetic judgment had found their finest expression. Otto's own thought along these lines is inextricably intertwined with that of Fries, and we will present it as such.

However one might translate the term *Ahndung* as it is used by Fries—and there is no consensus in this regard[73]—it implies, according to Otto, a feeling of "being in accord with the idea," and as such, is "nothing more or less than Plato's *'anamnesis'*."[74] "Through some resemblance or analogous relation, either accidental or more deeply founded, between some thing, some occurrence, and an idea, the idea is 'brought to remembrance,' is awakened, generally in obscure shape, and with it at the same time the corresponding emotion of the mind."[75] One example of this, Fries contends, can be found in the occurrence of miracles. In trying to understand how such occurrences "have always given the most potent impulse to the general awakening of religious feelings," we are left with no other explanation than that "the apparent mystery of some 'marvelous' occurrence arouses the 'memory' of the mystery of the supra-sensual in the absolute sense, which, latent in the feelings, now seems actively to participate in the actual course of events."[76] The miraculous event is subsumed under the idea, not through logical, categorical thought, but "by way of the immediate judgment of the feeling."[77] Our judgments about the beauty and sublimity of natural objects are of a similar nature, according to Fries and Otto. If we really *experience* (and not just taste) the sensible beauty of a flower or any other natural phenomenon, our aesthetic judgment about its beauty will involve a dim and inexpressible recognition of "ideal existence in general, without any determination of its particular and individual side."[78] The reminiscence, Otto states, "awakens within us moods and intuitions in which something of the essence and meaning of being is directly experienced, although it remains in the form of feeling, and cannot easily, if at all, find expression in definable ideas or clear statements."[79] We gain "an obscure comprehension of the unity and connection of true reality in the world of appearance, of this reality in its essential nature; and . . . of its teleology."[80] What Fries again has in mind here, Otto notes, "is in the truest sense a Platonic *anamnesis* of the idea."[81] It is a "third kind of knowledge"[82]—an "*a priori* principle"— which, according to both Fries and Otto, combines and unifies man's various ways of knowing.[83] In "undeveloped conceptions" resulting therefrom, and accompanying the aesthetic feeling, "we dimly see the eternal and true world of Spirit and Freedom . . . the world of the highest good," and sense something of the "mystery in religion"—"not the sort of mystery which would only exist for the uninitiated, which would be solved for the adept, but the sensible mystery of all existence in time as a whole—eternal reality breaking through the veil of temporal existence, to the unlocked heart."[84]

Fries, it should be noted, pressed this analogy between the aesthetic sense of beauty and the religious feeling of mystery so far that he has sometimes been accused of having reduced religion to aesthetics. Otto argues that it would be "more reasonable to censure [Fries] for elevating aesthetics into religion rather than for swamping religion in aesthetics."[85] For what Fries really meant, Otto contends, was that "in aesthetic impressions the profounder element, that which rises above 'frigid Taste' to the vivid sentiment of beauty and sublimity, is actually of a religious nature," in the sense that it "creates impressions on our mind in which the content of the intuitive perception far transcends the content of their 'concepts'" and leaves the mind under the religious "spell of mystery."[86] It should be noted, however, that at least in Otto's view, this still leaves room for a formal distinction between aesthetic and religious judgments.[87] Furthermore, Otto clearly is of the mind that the feeling resulting from the "contemplation of nature's harmonies and beauties" will not be the same for religious and non-religious individuals. "In a mind which is otherwise godless or undevout," he says, "it remains an indefinite, vacillating feeling, bringing with it nothing else."[88] "But in the religious mind," he concludes, "it immediately unites with what is akin to it or of similar nature, and becomes worship."[89]

Consistent with what psychologists say in general about the features common to all emotion,[90] Otto devoted much of his writing to a description of the physiological, behavioral, and mental aspects of the *sensus numinis*. The numinous feeling, he observed, is almost always accompanied by:(1) physiological changes, like the bristling of one's hair, the quaking of one's limbs, the creeping of one's flesh, or the running cold of one's blood;[91] (2) expressive behavior, like prostration of the body, flight, prayer, song, dance, and so forth;[92] and (3) mental states, like those of stupor, dread, fascination, humility, dependency, etc.[93] How exactly all these emotional elements might be related to each other is a matter of considerable debate in psychological circles.[94] But as far as Schleiermacher, Fries, and Otto themselves are concerned, there is no doubt that when they spoke of the religious sense as a feeling, what they primarily had in mind was its *cognitive* aspect. This is evidenced in the final analysis by the fact that more often than not they would define the feeling they were talking about as some "form of awareness": a "mode of knowing," a "cognition," an "inkling, surmise, or presage," an "intuition."[95] Some helpful hints about what it might mean to say that feeling involves a way of knowing have been provided by the more recent Kantian scholar, Ernst Cassirer, and a student of his, Suzanne Langer.

Cassirer made his comments in the context of his discussion of the difference between "mythic and religious consciousness." Underlying mythic and religious "symbolization" (the essential function of human consciousness), Cassirer observed, "is not a substratum of thought but of feeling."[96] But such feeling, he added, is not "entirely incoherent" or "bereft of sense or reason."[97] It involves a certain "consciousness," which, although antecedent to any "intuitive" (i.e., spatial/temporal, substantive) or "conceptual" (i.e., scientific and "relational") symbolization of reality,[98] is nonetheless cognitive. At the primitive level of "mythic consciousness," it consists of what might be called a "sympathy of the Whole,"[99] or the feeling for life as "an unbroken continuous whole which does not admit of any clean-cut and trenchant distinctions."[100] It is not that primitive man lacks the ability to appreciate empirically the differences of things, Cassirer noted.[101] But given the sympathetic nature of primitive consciousness, all such "differences are obliterated by a stronger feeling: the deep conviction of a fundamental and indelible solidarity of life that bridges over the multiplicity and variety of its single forms,"[102] with the result that the symbol and that to which it refers are experienced as being one and the same (e.g., name and person).[103] At this level of consciousness, "that which besets a man with sudden terror or wonder" (i.e., the divine), "still has an entirely impersonal, one might say 'anonymous,' character."[104]

The mythical "sympathy of the Whole" carried over, Cassirer claimed, into later stages of "religious consciousness," but "religious sympathy is of a different kind."[105] It "gives scope to a new feeling, that of individuality."[106] Spurred on by the natural tendency of language "to divide, determine, and fixate,"[107] and inspired by the "principle of differentiation" inherent to the "division of labor,"[108] religious feeling gave rise to an awareness of particular manifestations of the divine (e.g., the "functional gods").[109] But with no less a tendency on the part of language "to generalize,"[110] there also surfaced in religious consciousness a sense of the "unity of the God-idea" and the notion of "Being that is unlimited by any particular manifestation."[111] From the mythic "realm of mere indeterminateness" there is a progression to the religious "realm of true generality."[112] Unlike mythic consciousness, which, because of its identification of the sign and signified, altogether "lack[ed] the category of the ideal,"[113] religious consciousness now "separate[s] the ideal from the real,"[114] and thereby recognizes sensuous images and signs as such—namely, as "means of expression which, though they reveal a determinate meaning, must necessarily remain inadequate to it, which 'point' to this meaning but never wholly exhaust it."[115] There is now the feeling that things and events signify not simply themselves, but "something 'other,' something transcendent,"[116] ultimately, the nameless Self that is Pure Being.[117] According to Cassirer, "it is especially the cult of mysticism" that nurtured this "dialectical" evolution of religious consciousness.[118] But "it is only in the history of modern philosophical idealism," and especially in the thinking of modern philosophers of religion such as Schleiermacher, Cassirer concluded, "that the new view of the 'symbol' that emerges in mysticism achieves its full intellectual form."[119]

In response to a question about how feelings can involve a way of knowing, Suzanne Langer cited J. E. Creighton to the effect that "feelings have definite forms, which become progressively articulated . . . [and serve] as an index of the mind's grasp of its object."[120] Music, which has an "undeniable connection with feeling," is a good example, she notes.[121] Its history is full of "more and more integrated, disciplined, and articulated forms."[122] What these "articulated forms" do is not so much to express the feeling of the artist composing or performing the work, or to stir the emotions of the audience listening to it, as to afford "logical expression" to one or another feeling in itself.[123] A composer "articulates subtle complexes of feeling that language cannot even name, let alone set forth."[124] "We are not talking nonsense," therefore, "when we say that a certain musical progression is significant, or that a given phrase lacks meaning, or a player's rendering fails to convey the import of a passage."[125] The music invites us to seek insight into the feelings that are symbolized.[126] All of this could be interpreted to mean merely that by listening to music we might learn something about the psychology of love, sorrow, or any other feeling. But Langer seems to be saying much more. What she seems to be saying is that through the symbolic form that music takes we are afforded a chance to grasp intuitively, for example, not only what it means to love (in the sense of identifying the various ingredients of such a feeling, like shared interests, affection, etc.), but also, and more importantly, what love "means," or, in other words, what it "tells" us about life. We come to see that to love is to "know" reality in a certain way. We catch a glimpse of the essential nature of love; we see love in its "eternal, infinite, and ideal" form.[127]

NOTES

[1] See Copleston, *History of Philosophy*, Volume I, Part II, 68–73; Volume 6, Part II, 77–80, 95–96.

[2] See, in general: Copleston, *Kant*, 143; H. W. Cassirer, *A Commentary on Kant's Critique of Judgment* (New York and London: Barnes and Noble, Inc., and Methuen and Co., Ltd., 1970), 26–27.

[3] H. Cassirer, *Commentary*, 178.

[4] I. Kant, *Critique of Pure Reason*, in *GB* 42:45.

[5] Copleston, *Kant*, 25, 9.

[6] *Ibid.*, 25, 11, 19, 27, 72, 76, 97.

[7] *Ibid.*, 26, 77, 94–100.

[8] *Ibid.*, 60, 76, 94, 97.

[9] See J. Baillie, *The Interpretation of Religion* (New York: Charles Scribner's Sons, 1928), 237.

[10] See my discussion of this point in Verkamp, *Evolution of Religion*, 170–174.

[11] Rudolf Otto, *The Idea of the Holy* (New York: Oxford University Press, 1958), 150.

[12] *Ibid.*

[13] Rudolf Otto, *Das Gefuehl des Ueberweltlichen* (Muenchen: C. H. Beck'sche Verlagsbuchhandlung, 1932), 6; Robert F. Davidson, *Rudolf Otto's Interpretation of Religion* (Princeton: Princeton University Press, 1947), 64,n23.

[14] Friedrich Schleiermacher, *On Religion, Speeches to Its Cultured Despisers* (New York: Harper and Row, 1958), 49–50, 67, 26–118; R. Otto, *Religious Essays* (London: Oxford University Press, 1931), 68–77.

[15] R Otto, *The Philosophy of Religion* (London: Williams and Norgate, 1931), 22–23.

[16] *Ibid.*, 23; Otto, *Idea of the Holy*, 148.

[17] Otto, *Philosophy of Religion*, 100–101, 131–144; Jakob Friedrich Fries, *Dialogues on Morality and Religion* (Totowa, N.J.: Barnes and Noble, 1982), 209–244; J. F. Fries, *Knowledge, Belief and Aesthetic Sense*, edited and introduced by Frederick Gregory, translated by Kent Richter (Cologne: Juergen Dinter Verlag fuer Philosophie, 1989), 93–157.

[18] Otto, *Idea of the Holy*, xvi, 125.

[19] See Noam Chomsky's comments in regard to Leibniz, in Stephen P. Stich, *Innate Ideas* (Berkeley, Los Angeles, and London: University of California Press, 1975), 92, 101,n3.

[20] A. E. Taylor, *Plato: The Man and His Work* (New York: The Dial Press, 1936), 136, 138, 188.

[21] *Ibid.*, 138,n2, 188.

[22] *Ibid.*, 136, 187, 188.

[23] See Otto, *Philosophy of Religion*, 135.

[24] See Hannah Arendt, *The Life of the Mind*, Volume One, *Thinking* (New York and London: Harcourt Brace Jovanovich, 1978), 114–125.

[25] Taylor, *Plato*, 136.

[26] Otto, *Philosophy of Religion*, 143,n1; see also *Ibid.*, 93, 113, 133, 134; Otto, *Idea of the Holy*, 40, 147–148.

[27] Cassirer, *Commentary*, 179, 198.

[28] *Ibid.*, 179.

[29] *Ibid.*, 178; Copleston, *Kant*, 142–146.

[30] Cassirer, *Commentary*, 152, 198.

[31] I. Kant, *The Critique of Judgement*, GB 42:542.

[32] *Ibid.*

[33] *Ibid.*

[34] *Ibid.*

[35] *Ibid.*, 542–543.

[36] Cassirer, *Commentary*, 299.

[37] *Ibid.*, 198; Copleston, *Kant*, 142, 152.

[38] See Otto, *Idea of the Holy*, 146, 147–148; *Philosophy of Religion*, 15, 22–24; Otto, *Essays*, 68–77. Richard Niebuhr agrees that in the *Speeches* Schleiermacher identifies the feeling of "harmony with the All" or the "awareness that the infinite is immediately present in the finite self and that the self is a unique statement of the universal concourse of being" by the "name of feeling and again of intuition," but that later, "in the *Christmas Eve*, he speaks of the Christian feeling and mood, in his philosophical ethics of feeling as a subjective knowing; in the dialectics it is the representation of the transcendent ground of being, and in *The Christian Faith* he defines religion as an immediate self-consciousness and a feeling of absolute dependence" (R. Niebuhr, "Friedrich Schleiermacher," in *A Handbook of Christian Theologians* eds., Martin E. Marty and Dean G. Peerman [Cleveland and New York: The World Publishing Company, 1967] 28–29). "What I understand by religious feeling," Schleiermacher is quoted by Richard Niebuhr as having said in one of his letters to Dr. Luecke, "by no means derives from conception, rather it is the original expression of an immediate existence-relationship" (R. Niebuhr, *Schleiermacher on Christ and Religion* [New York: Charles Scribner's Sons, 1964], 183). "*The Christian Faith* makes this relational dimension of religion even clearer," Niebuhr concludes, "when it proceeds to interpret this feeling as a feeling of the 'whence' of personal existence and stipulates that here one has precisely the datum to which we refer when we speak of being in relation to God" (*Ibid.*).

[39] Otto, *Essays*, 74–75.

[40] *Ibid.*, 75–76.

[41] *Ibid.*, 76–77; Otto, *Idea of the Holy*, 147; R. Otto, *Naturalism and Religion* (London: Williams and Norgate, 1913), 75–76.

[42] Otto, *Idea of the Holy*, 146–147.

[43] See Otto, *Idea of the Holy*, 150–154; Otto, *Philosophy of Religion*, 131, 135; Otto, *Naturalism*, 24; and especially, Otto, *Gefuehl des Uberweltlichen*, 327–333.

[44] Otto, *Naturalism*, 24–28.

[45] H. B. Nisbet, *Goethe and the Scientific Tradition* (London: Institute of Germanic Studies, 1972), 48.

[46] Otto, *Naturalism*, 25.

[47] See Nisbet, *Goethe*, 17–19, 36, 39–44, 46, 47, 51; Alan P. Cottrell, *Goethe's View of Evil* (Edinburg: Floris Books, 1982), 227, 240, 241; Willy Hartner, "Goethe and the Natural Sciences," in Victor Lange, ed., *Goethe: A Collection of Critical Essays* (Englewood Cliffs, N.J.: Prentice-Hall, Inc., 1968), 152; Ernst Busch, *Goethe's Religion* (Tuebingen: Furche-Verlag, 1949), 344.

[48] Otto, *Gefuehl des Uberweltlichen*, 329.

[49] *Ibid.*, 328.

[50] *Ibid.*

[51] *Ibid.*, 327, 328.

[52] *Ibid.*, 328.

[53] See Copleston, *Kant*, 26, 72, 95, 142.

[54] See *NCE* 14: 389–390, 391; and *Infra*, Chapter V, n.108.

[55] See Copleston, *Kant*, 26, 72, 95, 142.

[56] See Cottrell, *Goethe's View of Evil*, 223; Robert Barth, S.J., *Coleridge and Christian Doctrine* (Cambridge, MA.: Harvard University Press, 1969), 16–18; E.D. Hirsch, Jr., *Wordsworth and Schelling* (New Haven: Yale University Press, 1960), 130; Martin S. Day, *History of English Literature*, 1660–1837 (Garden City: N.Y.: Doubleday and Company, Inc., 1963), 368, 437; Gay Wilson Allen, "A New Look at Emerson and

Science," in Robert E. Burkholder and Joel Myerson, *Critical Essays on Ralph Waldo Emerson* (Boston: G. K. Hall and Co., 1983), 442; Richard Ruland, ed., *Twentieth Century Interpretations of Walden* (Englewood Cliffs, N.J.: Prentice-Hall, Inc., 1968), 36.

[57] See Lange, *Goethe*, 164–166; Robert Dickens, *Thoreau: The Complete Individualist* (New York: Exposition Press, 1974), 17–39.

[58] See Day, *English Literature*, 368–369; Hirsch, *Wordsworth and Schelling*, 98–146.

[59] Dorothy M. Emmet, "Coleridge on the Growth of the Mind," in Kathleen Coburn, *Coleridge: A Collection of Critical Essays* (Englewood-Cliffs, N.J.: Prentice-Hall, Inc., 1967), 168.

[60] Nisbet, *Goethe*, 17–19, 36, 39–44, 46, 47, 51.

[61] *Ibid.*, 57.

[62] *Ibid.*, 59, 60.

[63] See Lange, *Goethe*, 165–166; Cottrell, *Goethe's View of Evil*, 221–223; Busch, *Goethe's Religion*, 344–345.

[64] Nisbet, *Goethe*, 8–11.

[65] *Ibid.*, 21; Robert D. Richardson, Jr., *Henry Thoreau: A Life of the Mind* (Berkeley: University of California Press, 1986), 376–379.

[66] Day, *English Literature*, 368; Nisbet, *Goethe*, 45.

[67] See Hartner, "Goethe and the Natural Sciences," 145; Cottrell, *Goethe's View of Evil*, 221.

[68] See Nisbet, *Goethe*, 41–42, 56, 67; Barth, *Coleridge*, 20–23; Dickens, *Thoreau*, 44–45.

[69] See Nisbet, *Goethe*, 42.

[70] Allen, "Emerson and Science," 442; Cottrell, *Goethe's View of Evil*, 232; Emmet, "Coleridge on the Growth of the Mind," 171; Edmund A. Schofield and Robert C. Baron, eds., *Thoreau's World and Ours* (Golden, Colorado: North American Press, 1993), 39.

[71] Cottrell, *Goethe's View of Evil*, 227, 240, 241; Frederick B. Wahr, *Emerson and Goethe* (Folcroft, Pa.: The Folcroft Press, Inc., 1969), 31.

[72] Cottrell, *Goethe's View of Evil*, 227; Dickens, *Thoreau*, 7–16.

[73] For a discussion of the translation of *Ahndung*, see Otto, *Philosophy of Religion*, 11; Fries, *Dialogues*, xv–xvi; Fries, *Knowledge, Belief and Aesthetic Sense*, 9–10.

[74] Otto, *Philosophy of Religion*, 93, 35; Otto, *Naturalism*, 75.

[75] Otto, *Philosophy of Religion*, 135.

[76] *Ibid.*, 136.

[77] *Ibid.*

[78] *Ibid.*, 140–141; Otto, *Naturalism*, 75.

[79] Otto, *Naturalism*, 75.

[80] Otto, *Philosophy of Religion*, 141; Otto, *Naturalism*, 77–84.

[81] Otto, *Philosophy of Religion*, 93; Otto, *Naturalism*, 75.

[82] Fries identified three different ways of discovering the truth about reality. *Wissen* or "knowing" provides us, he says, with "concepts" by which we understand the "finite" in nature (Fries, *Knowledge, Belief and Aesthetic Sense*, 95). But, however important such knowledge might be, he adds, it cannot capture the "higher ends" of human history. Only "ideas" can do that (*Ibid.*, 73–75). All that is "high and noble" in reason dwells only in ideas, and is born only from ideas. It is reason that gives rise to the ideas of God, freedom, immortality of the soul, etc. (*Ibid.*, 74). In *Glaube* ("Belief"), we lay claim to the truth of such ideas (*Ibid.*, 95). We "believe" in the eternal, in the "purpose and

finality" of Nature, etc. But the ideas themselves contain no positive knowledge about God and the world. They are totally "negative," in the sense that they are derived "from the negation of the limitations of the finite" (*Ibid.*, 95). Thus, for example, "all the ideas through which we gain a belief in the higher world order—the ideas of immortality, freedom and deity—only arise for us because we think away the incompletability and limitedness from the being of things before our eyes (*Ibid.*, 96). Or, again, "in the idea of the absolute, the unconditioned, or in the idea of the elimination of the limitation (of natural knowledge), we rise to the idea of being-in-itself"(*Ibid.*, 74). What this implies is that just as the "concepts" of understanding are confined to the finite, so the ideas of reason and belief are not valid in the finite; they are without any sensible intuitions, without any images (*Ibid.*, 95). Neither understanding, therefore, nor reason, can grasp "the eternal in the finite" (*Ibid.*). For the truth of the latter to be apprehended, there must be a third way of "claiming the truth," and that third way is *Ahndung* or "aesthetic sense" (*Ibid.*, 95–97). One cannot "understand" the presence of the eternal, nor can one grasp it in the ideals of belief; one can only feel or aesthetically sense the idea of a higher world (i.e., the totality, the unity of Nature; its purposiveness and finality) "in the beauty and sublimity of Nature" (*Ibid.*, 96). "All positive cognition of the eternal" is referred back "to a pure inexpressible feeling (*Ibid.*). See also Fries, *Dialogues*, 209–244.

[83]   Otto, *Philosophy of Religion*, 100–101; Copleston, *Kant*, 142.

[84]   Otto, *Philosophy of Religion*, 93, 101.

[85]   *Ibid.*, 133.

[86]   *Ibid.*, 134, 93.

[87]   *Ibid.*, 136.

[88]   Otto, *Naturalism*, 77.

[89]   *Ibid.*

[90]   See Sdorow, *Psychology*, 466–480.

[91]   Otto, *Idea of the Holy*, 16.

[92]   *Ibid.*, 81.

[93]   *Ibid.*, 13–15, 20–21, 31–40, 84.

[94]   See Sdorow, *Psychology*, 480–490.

[95]   See, for example, Otto, *Idea of the Holy*, 145–150.

[96]   E. Cassirer, *An Essay on Man* (New Haven: Yale University Press, 1956), 81.

[97]   *Ibid.*

[98]   *EP* 3:45.

[99]   Cassirer, *Man*, 94.

[100]   *Ibid.*, 81; E. Cassirer, *The Philosophy of Symbolic Forms*, Volume 2: *Mythic Thought* (New Haven and London: Yale University Press, 1955), 38.

[101]   Cassirer, *Man*, 82.

[102]   *Ibid.*

[103]   *Ibid.*, 81.

[104]   E. Cassirer, *Language and Myth* (New York: Dover Publications, Inc., 1946), 71, 74.

[105]   Cassirer, *Man*, 95.

[106]   *Ibid.*, 96.

[107]   Cassirer, *Language and Myth*, 73.

[108]   Cassirer, *Man*, 96.

[109]   *Ibid.*, 97.

[110]   Cassirer, *Language and Myth*, 73.

[111]   *Ibid.*

[112]   *Ibid.*, 74.

[113] Cassirer, *Mythic Thought*, 38.

[114] *Ibid.*, 38, 238.

[115] *Ibid.*, 239.

[116] *Ibid.*, 252.

[117] Cassirer, *Language and Myth*, 75–78.

[118] *Ibid.*, 74.

[119] Cassirer, *Mythic Thought*, 258–260.

[120] S. Langer, *Philosophy in a New Key* (New York: The New American Library, 1953), 81.

[121] *Ibid.*, 175.

[122] *Ibid.*

[123] *Ibid.*, 174–180.

[124] *Ibid.*, 180.

[125] *Ibid.*, 82.

[126] *Ibid.*, 181.

[127] *Ibid.*, 179.

CHAPTER FOUR

Omnipotent Intentionality/ Preapprehension

Another way of trying to explain the religious sense of mystery as a product of an animated brain (or a brain, in other words, that is under the formal influence of the human soul) can be found in the claim by some modern, so-called Transcendental Thomists that all of human knowledge is grounded in an "anticipatory pre-apprehension" of God as the "mysterious horizon of Being." Among the major proponents of Transcendental Thomism in recent times have been Karl Rahner, Emerich Coreth, Bernard Lonergan, and Joseph Donceel. Our focus in this chapter will be mainly on the thought of Karl Rahner. The writings of the other Transcendental Thomists, not all of whom, of course, agree on every point, will be referred to only to help elucidate Rahner's own line of thought.

Transcendental Thomism originated with an attempt earlier in this century by a Belgium philosopher, named Joseph Maréchal, to reconcile Kant's transcendental reflection on human knowledge with the meta-physical realism of Thomas Aquinas.[1] Not surprisingly, therefore, the Transcendental Thomists usually begin their discussion with a point shared by both Thomas and Kant,[2] namely, the rejection of common sense empiricism and its implication of naive realism. According to such a picture theory of knowledge, "knowing is identical with looking, objectivity is identical with what can be seen, and reality is identical with what is there."[3] It implies, in other words, that the human intellect is like a mirror that is totally passive and receptive, and the known, as an image or copy of the object it reflects, is something, therefore, which comes entirely from the outside.[4] In the view of Transcendental Thomists, however, human knowledge is far more complex.[5] And to avoid the skepticism that inevitably results from reliance upon sense experience alone, it is necessary, they say, to take into more adequate account the active role of the intellect.

Kant, of course, had clearly recognized this point also. Having been awakened from his dogmatic slumber by a reading of Hume's skeptical appraisal of sense knowledge, and determined to recover an absolute ("universal and necessary") basis for science, Kant, as is well known, concluded that it is not so much the object that determines the knowing subject, as it is the knowing subject who determines the object of knowledge.[6] And much of his subsequent effort was directed toward trying to show exactly what it is that the mind contributes to our knowledge of the objects of our experience. Eschewing any theory of innate ideas or intellectual intuition by which the human intellect might be thought to bypass sense knowledge altogether and enjoy some kind of direct and immediate apprehension of reality, Kant proceeded instead to demonstrate through his "transcendental method" that what the mind contributes are certain "forms of judgment," or "categories," by which, and by which alone, as the *a priori* conditions of their intelligibility, the data of sense experience can be organized and rendered intelligible.

For all its merit, Kant's critical idealism did not really succeed, the Transcendental Thomists argued, in overcoming the skeptical dimensions of Hume's radical empiricism. Because of its exclusive focus upon the "conceptualist" dimension of human knowing and neglect of the knowing act itself, the only immediate contact with objects provided by the Kantian approach, they said, was through sensible intuition,[7] with the result that the transcendental knowledge it delivered was, in the final analysis, "illusory"; it provided knowledge of only the "phenomenon," or, in other words, of only the object as it appeared to the knowing subject, not of the object in itself (the noumenon),[8] and it rendered any ideas about the spiritual realm, the so-called transcendental ideas of God, etc., merely "regulative."[9] Kant's failure in this regard to reach a more "realistic metaphysics," the Transcendental Thomists claimed, could be compensated for by closer attention to the "dynamic" structure of the human intellect.[10] Johann Gottlieb Fichte, they thought, had provided a hint of such a "spiritual dynamism" with his suggestion that because of the human subject's "intellectual intuition of his own spiritual activity of knowing and willing, man has an awareness of the latter as consisting fundamentally of a "striving toward the Infinite."[11] What this implied, according to the Transcendental Thomists, was that "if the mind's real striving toward the Infinite Absolute is one of the *a priori* conditions of the speculative reason's objective judgments, [then] God's real existence is an *a priori* condition of possibility for every categorical judgment of the speculative reason."[12] And inspired by the writings of Maurice Blondel and Pierre Rousselot about the teleological thrust of Thomas' "intellectualism,"[13] they came to see that such a conclusion had actually been implied by Thomas' contention that man's analogous knowledge of God is grounded in "the drive of the active intellect to the Infinite God."[14] To "thematize" and "make explicit" this spiritual dynamism of the human intellect was, they concluded, the "main task of the metaphysician."[15]

In trying to meet that task, Rahner undertook a thorough investigation and reinterpretation of Thomas' views on the "cogitative power" of the human intellect. Medieval philosophers had generally conceived of such a cogitative power as an extension into the human realm of what, in an earlier chapter, we have seen them referring to as the "estimative power" in brute animals.[16] Through its use, they were inclined to say, humans might be able to evaluate the "suitability" of one or another particular good.[17] In Rahner's interpretation of Thomas, it came to be viewed as something of a "bridge between the intellect and the senses," on which the "universal" and "necessary" dimension of the immaterial intellect could meet and unite with the "particular and contingent" elements provided by the material senses, and deliver an "intelligible" image, or an image, in other words, that would, so to speak, be "suitable" to the natural "intentions" of the intellect.[18] As the "center" of the intellect's activity and passivity ("the center in which spirit and sensibility, which emanated from the spirit, merge together in one human knowing"), the cogitative sense is said to be the "locus" of both "abstraction" and "conversion to the phantasm."[19] Or, more accurately, the "*act* of the cogitative sense is objectively identical with the conversion to the phantasm,"[20] and the "conversion to the phantasm is nothing other than the illumination of the phantasm by the light of the agent intellect."[21] The cogitative sense, in still other words, is the power of the human spirit, through the union of its intellect and senses, "to apprehend the individual *as* existing in the *common* nature."[22] In and apart from the intellect (as in brute animals), the senses could not "differentiate" (i.e., evaluate the "suitability") "between the individual as such and the common nature," and the intellect, without the senses, could not grasp the individual.[23] But together, in the cogitative sense, "the individuality and the common nature are given in a differentiated unity."[24] To that extent, Rahner states, the cogitative sense can also be equated with the "power of judgment," since "in the German philosophical tradition this word [Judgment, *Urteilskraft*] designates the power to think of the particular as contained under the universal."[25]

Traditionally, this "act" of the cogitative sense, involving both abstraction and conversion to the phantasm, had been explained by many of Thomas' interpreters, as a two step process, whereby the intellect, through an act of "simple apprehension," "extracts" the "universal" from the singular, concrete, material image by dropping all its particular features and retaining only what it has in common with things of its kind, and then referring the "concept" (the "expressed species" consciously fashioned by the mind out of the "intelligible species" unconsciously "impressed" on the mind) back to the object "by affirming its adequation to external reality."[26] But in addition to implying that the human intellect is entirely passive, that the intellect already knows all the features among which it must choose, and that intellect and senses have separate representations of the known,[27] such an interpretation gives rise to the notion of "being" as merely "the *summum genus* of the logicians," or, as Hegel put it, "the emptiest of terms precisely because it is the commonest, [signifying] the very least that can be thought of anything."[28]

Thomas avoided such difficulties, Rahner wrote, by recognizing that "conversion to the phantasm and abstraction are moments of a single process and are inseparably related to each other in a relationship of reciprocal priority."[29] Although each may be said to enjoy some "logical priority" over the other,[30] they are, in reality, "two sides of the one process."[31] "The conversion to the phantasm is not merely a turning of the spirit to sensibility which is logically prior to the actual knowledge of the universal and makes it possible, but is precisely that movement of the spirit in which the sensible content is informed, as it were, by the *a priori* structure of the spirit, by its 'light,' that is, is seen within the absolute being which the spirit preapprehends, and is known in its universality."[32] There are not, in other words, "two representations of the same object," but only one, namely, "the image produced by the senses." But this sense image is "potentially intelligible," and its "potentiality" is spontaneously "actualized" by the intellect, "not by the mere dropping of its individual features . . . but by the addition of some new element," namely, the element of "being."[33] This is possible, Rahner contends, because, according to Thomas, the human intellect is "not a purely passive faculty in the formation of ideas, but contributes something of its own."[34] What the intellect contributes is the "original self-presence of the subject."[35] Unlike God, who, as "pure Spirit," is "supreme and fully luminous self-awareness,"[36] man, as a material creature whose knowledge is always dependent upon sensibility,[37] is never, Rahner notes, entirely "present to himself."[38] Still, in the "original awareness" of his own knowing act, man can, Rahner argues, have a "pre-apprehension [*Vorgriff*]" of himself as a subject that "is fundamentally and by its very nature pure openness for absolutely everything, for being as such."[39] Rahner often refers to this "original subjective consciousness" as a "transcendental experience."[40] It is "transcendental," he says, "because it belongs to the necessary and inalienable structures of the knowing subject itself, and because it consists precisely in the transcendence beyond any particular group of possible objects or of categories."[41] It is an "experience," he adds, "because this knowledge, unthematic but ever-present, is a moment within and a condition of possibility for every concrete experience of any and every object."[42] In other words, the "anticipation of being" generated by the knowing subject's becoming present to itself "forms an antecedent law governing what and how something can become manifest to the knowing subject"; it is an *a priori* condition of all human knowledge.[43] Only in the "light" of, or on the "horizon" of, such an "anticipation of being" can the reality of the sensible object be grasped.[44]

That human consciousness does, in fact, enjoy a fundamental orientation toward "the absolute and the incomprehensible" realm of "Being," and what, more precisely, it consists of, can best be demonstrated, according to Rahner, Lonergan, and other Transcendental Thomists, in terms of what Aristotle and Thomas Aquinas described as man's innate "desire to know" and the insatiable "questioning" arising therefrom.[45]

Given the material creature that he is, man, Rahner observes, is "not [unlike God] the unquestioning and unquestioned infinity of reality."[46] He is rather "the spirit who experiences himself as spirit in that he does not experience himself as pure spirit."[47] As such, Rahner says, man is by nature "the question which rises up before him."[48] "Prior to any insights, any concepts, any words," Lonergan notes, man finds himself confronted with a sense of "wonder . . . that desire to understand, that constitutes the primordial 'Why'? . . . the pure question."[49] "To doubt [the knowing subject's] questioning," Lonergan writes in an appreciative commentary on Coreth's metaphysics, "is to involve oneself in a counter position, and so questioning is beyond the doubter's capacity to doubt coherently."[50]

No better "starting point" for metaphysics can be found, therefore, than in the "question about the question."[51]

What is found upon analyzing the essence of questioning, we are told, is that "the condition of the possibility of any and all questions is an awareness that goes beyond the already known to an unknown to be known."[52] To limit questioning, therefore, would again "land one in a counter position," for "to propose a limit to questioning is to raise the question of the legitimacy of asking questions beyond the limit; and raising this question is already beyond the limit."[53] Just as "anyone who says objectively and thematically that there is no truth affirms this statement to be true," so, Rahner argues, anyone denying "an unlimited openness of the spirit to absolutely everything implicitly posits and affirms such an openness."[54] "For a subject which knows itself to be finite, and in its knowledge is not just unknowing with regard to the limited nature of the possibility of its objects, has already transcended its finiteness."[55] Even the "suspicion" of an "intrinsic limitation of the subject" already posits the "preapprehension [of everything]" as "going beyond the suspicion."[56] Not only, then, is man a question; he is also, as Rahner says, "a question to which there is no answer."[57] Lonergan adds along Augustinian lines that by participating in "the Uncreated Light that is God Himself," humans enjoy "an intentional omnipotence . . . a capacity to ask questions about everything."[58] The "unrestricted desire to know" gives rise to ever "further questions that take [man] beyond the defined limits of particular issues."[59] "Every answer is always just the beginning of a new question," Rahner comments.[60] "The more answers man can discover," therefore, "the more is the infinite horizon of human questioning" experienced as receding "further and further."[61] "We would know everything about everything," Lonergan adds, "the whole universe in all its multiplicity and concreteness, *omnia, to pan*, and, in that concrete and comprehensive sense, being."[62]

That the "term" of such radical questioning by man is the positive fullness of being, and not "nothingness," is evident, Rahner claims, from the fact that while humans do on occasion experience "emptiness," "inner fragility," and even "absurdity," they also have moments of "hope" and "freedom."[63] The unity of such experiences under the influence of an "ultimate and primordial movement" defies any radically "dualistic" interpretation of ultimate reality, so even while acknowledging the possibility of an "absolute being" that "establishes limits and boundaries outside of itself" (ultimately through a "graceful" process of "making itself manifest,") one is left with the conclusion that "the ultimate ground of everything is not empty nothingness," but the positive fullness of infinite reality."[64]

In referring to this positive term and source of man's transcendental experience, Rahner himself will sometimes follow what he calls the "venerable tradition of the whole of western philosophy," and give it the name of "being as such," or "absolute being," or "being in an absolute sense," or the "ground of being."[65] But because of "the risk that many contemporaries can hear the word 'being' only as an empty and subsequent abstraction from the multiple experience of the individual realities which encounter us directly,"[66] we would do better, Rahner suggests, "to call the term and source of our transcendence 'the [holy][67] mystery,'"[68] or, in other words, that which is "nameless,"[69] "indefinable," "ineffable," "incomprehensible."[70] As such, he continues, the term and source of our transcendence can also "be called 'God',"[71] for, expressing as it does in its present form "the whole in its unity and totality," it is precisely to the "ineffable one," "the nameless one," "the silent one," that the word God refers.[72] The word "mystery," with the added qualification of "holy," can be shown, in other words, to be "identical with the word God."[73] Or to arrive at the same conclusion from the opposite direction, the term "God," according to Rahner, is the ultimate "*Urwort*," the greatest of those "great words," which, unlike "the fabricated, technical, useful words" by which we try to control our world by dividing and "fencing things off" from each other, are "like sea shells in which, no matter how small they themselves are, the ocean of Infinity thunders,"[74] because in them "everything that is, is interwoven with everything else, "and the "mystery" of the "unity in multiplicity, of the essential in the phenomenal, the wholeness in the part, and the partiality in the whole," is "conjured up."[75]

If, therefore, the transcendental experience of asking questions about "everything" presupposes a "preapprehension" of "the whole in its unity and totality," we have reason to conclude also, Rahner says, that there is some kind of knowledge of "God" present in that same experience.[76] But what is the nature of such knowledge? In the first place, Rahner observes, it is of an *a posteriori* sort. It is such, he says, "insofar as man's transcendental experience of his subjectivity takes place only in his encounter with the world and especially with other people."[77] It does not, in other words, provide the knowing subject with any "intuitive" knowledge of God of the sort Orestes Brownson and other so-called "ontologists" liked to claim.[78] "God," as the "term and source of transcendence," is present, Rahner notes, "only in the mode of otherness and distance," and "can never be approached directly, never be grasped immediately."[79] This should not be taken to mean, however, Rahner cautions, that we can "look out into the world with a neutral faculty of knowledge and then think that we can discover God there directly or indirectly among the realities that present themselves to us objectively, or that we can prove his existence indirectly."[80] We must remember, in other words, that such knowledge of God as we are talking about here is "transcendental,"[81] Rahner writes, in the sense that it "is a permanent existential of man as a spiritual subject," and as such "grounds all of his knowledge and all of his conscious activity."[82]

As "transcendental," such knowledge of God, Rahner adds, is also "original," in the sense of being an "*Ureinsicht*" that originates and grounds every other way of knowing by capturing those mysterious dimensions of the whole of reality that will forever escape rational definition.[83] To that extent, it must also be described as being "pre-reflective," "unthematic," "anonymous," "preconceptual," and ulti-mately, "passive and receptive." It is "prereflective," Rahner says, in the sense that although metaphysical reflection on the knowing subject's "self-presence," or theological reflection on the nature and existence of God, may be "altogether necessary and required," such reflection can never be anything more than an "elaboration of a more original knowledge, and can never "recapture" the latter entirely.[84] It (the "pre-apprehension of God") is "unthematic," Rahner says, in the sense that it is "not the kind of knowledge in which one grasps an object which happens to present itself directly or indirectly from outside."[85] Rather, "it goes on, so to speak, behind the back of the knower, who is looking away from himself and at the [sensible] object."[86]

Although susceptible to elaboration along mythological, symbolic, and analogical lines through the experience of divine revelation and the encounter with human death, freedom, love, and other natural phenomena, in and of itself, the "preapprehension of God carries no positive, concrete, and determinate content."[87] It is "preconceptual," Rahner states repeatedly, because "the original experience of God is not an encounter with an individual object alongside of other objects."[88] "To define [something] conceptually," he explains, would be "to objectify it, to understand it as one object among other objects,"[89] and although we do that all the time in our "manipulative dealings" with other entities, "there is no such way of knowing God."[90] The "mysterious and the incomprehensible" can "never be situated within our system of coordinates, and can never be defined by being distinguished from something else." "The ultimate measure cannot itself be measured . . . the infinite expanse which can and does encompass everything cannot itself be encompassed."[91] It may very well happen, Rahner concedes, that some "concept of God" will follow from our "original experience," and certainly, he says, "a person ought to avoid the effort involved in this process of reflexive conceptualization."[92] But all "such conceptualizing" will "remain true," he hastens to add, "only to the extent that, in this act of defining and expressing objectively the term of transcendence as the act's condition of possibility, once again an act of transcendence towards the infinite term of this transcendence takes place."[93] "All metaphysical ontology about God must return again and again to its source,"[94] and recognize anew that what one is talking about is the "mystery" which defies final "definition" and is ultimately "nameless."[95] This is what Rahner means by suggesting that the "preapprehension of God" is "anonymous."[96]

In regard to any subsequent "conceptualization," Rahner makes another important point that explains why he thinks that our "original" knowledge of God is also, in the final analysis, "passive and receptive." "It would be the greatest misunderstanding, a misunderstanding which would lose all connection with the original experience," he writes, "if this term [of our transcendentality] were explained as something in the mind, as an *idea* which human thought established by its own creation," and whose "existential import" would subsequently have to be demonstrated.[97] "Being" is given in the very transcendental experience of one's subjectivity.[98] But this "becoming present of the knowing subject to itself" as an entity that is "open to everything" is not a matter of "the subject creating its own unlimited space as though it had absolute power over being, but it is the infinite horizon of being making itself manifest."[99] "The term of transcendence opens our transcendence; it is not established by us and by our own power as though we were absolute subjects."[100] Far from identifying itself as an "absolute" or "divine" subject,[101] or the product of raw "intentionality" apart from its term,[102] therefore, the knowing subject, Rahner will insist, "recognizes itself as a transcendence which has been bestowed upon it, which is grounded in mystery, and is not at its own disposal."[103] In a word, the "silent One" creates its own "listener," not vice-versa.[104] And so, in the end, the "preapprehension of God" is, according to Rahner, "at once both natural knowledge, and knowledge in grace."[105]

Lonergan, it may be noted in passing, arrived at a similar conclusion about the "anticipatory awareness" of God resulting from man's experience of the "spiritual dynamism" of himself as a knowing subject. That such a transcendental experience does in fact involve some kind of "pre-knowledge" of God was at least implied by Lonergan in his discussion of "God as the supreme fulfilment" of the "transcendental notions" of "being, truth, goodness and value" which operate in all our knowing and govern the insights and judgments we make about the sensible data of experience.[106] "God," in other words, might be "anticipated" in a non-conceptual way as the "supreme intelligence, truth, reality, righteousness, goodness," toward which all human striving (intellectual and volitional) is directed.[107]

A more explicit account of what is to be understood by the "anticipatory awareness" of "God" was provided by Lonergan in the context of his argument that "God exists because the real is completely intelligible."[108] In response to an objection from David Burrell against this argument on grounds that "we cannot know complete intelligibility," Lonergan observed that "between not knowing and knowing there is the process of coming to know."[109] "It is neither ignorance nor knowledge but the dynamic intermediary between ignorance and knowledge. It is the conscious movement away from ignorance and towards knowledge."[110] "That process," Lonergan concludes, as we have already seen in his analysis of "questioning," "is intentional."[111] "Whenever one asks a genuine question, one does not know the answer. Still, one does intend, desire, ask for the answer; one is able to tell when one gets an appropriate answer; and one is able to judge whether the appropriate answer is also correct."[112] The process, in other words, is "not blind": "It is aware of itself as a going beyond the given, the incompletely known."[113]

While, therefore, it may be true that "we have no immediate knowledge of complete intelligibility," it remains the case that our human intelligence "intends" complete intelligibility.[114] And if God, as Pure Being, can be identified with "complete intelligibility," then, Lonergan concludes, we have reason to think that we have an "intentional" awareness of God's presence.[115] Like Rahner, however, Lonergan will also insist that "God is not and cannot be an object in the etymological sense, in the Kantian sense, in the sense acceptable to a logical atomism, positivism, or empiricism."[116] "We have no immediate knowledge of God," Lonergan states unequivocally.[117] But "object" can also be understood as that which is "intended in questioning."[118] And even "if God cannot be an object in the etymological or Kantian or equivalent meanings of the word 'object', it would be only a fallacy,"

Lonergan argued, " to conclude that he cannot be an object in the quite different meaning just indicated," namely, as an "object to which we dynamically are orientated by our questions but which we only partially know."[119] Finally, again like Rahner, Lonergan will also acknowledge that while our "intentional awareness" of God is part of the *a priori* structure of the human intellect, it is *a posteriori* to the extent of being generated by the knowing subject's experience of itself in the world, and to the extent of relying upon sensations, perceptions, images, etc., for its determinate content.[120]

Rahner and Lonergan both acknowledge that it can and does often happen that humans take a rather bourgeois attitude toward life and try "to evade the mysterious infinity" toward which all questioning points, by devoting themselves exclusively to the concrete world of "work and activity in the categorical realm of space and time."[121] They busy themselves in the study of the physical, biological, chemical, economic, political, and other particular dimensions of experience to such an extent that they take no heed of the ultimate question about "man as a unity and a whole."[122] Or, in a skeptical mood, they dismiss the question about the meaning of it all as "unanswerable" and "meaningless."[123] To counter such an attitude, Rahner says, such individuals might be reminded that if the word "God" disappears, and questions are raised about "the single whole of reality" or about "the single whole of [man's] own existence," individuals could "regress to the level of a clever animal," and the whole of the human race could die "a collective death and regress back into a colony of unusually resourceful animals."[124]

Toward the same end, Rahner notes, theoretical "proofs for the existence of God" could be proffered to convince skeptics of the reasonableness of religious faith.[125] But all such efforts are doomed to fail, he adds, unless they are "intended to mediate a reflexive awareness of the fact that man always and inevitably has to do with God in his intellectual and spiritual existence, whether he reflects upon it or not, and whether he freely accepts it or not."[126] Only when the listener can be shown "that he already has something to do with this question [of God, of total meaning, etc.]," can theology and philosophy expect to have its talk about God taken seriously by modern man.[127] But that is exactly what Rahner, Lonergan, and all the Transcendental Thomists have in mind to show, namely, that if man is honest with himself, he cannot help but acknowledge that he is "an unlimited question without its own answer,"[128] and that nothing is more "self-evident in human life," therefore, than "mystery in its incomprehensibility,"[129] than "the silent question which goes beyond everything which has already been mastered and controlled."[130] The "unrestricted reach" of human "intentionality," Lonergan notes, "cannot be ignored."[131] "The atheist may pronounce it empty. The agnostic may urge that he finds his investigation has been inconclusive. The contemporary humanist will refuse to allow the question to arise. But their negations presuppose the spark in our clod, our native orientation to the divine."[132] The "trick" then, for anyone interested in keeping modern people in touch with "God," is to challenge them to inquire into their own inquisitive nature, for it is "only when one begins to ask about asking itself, and to think about thinking itself, only when one turns his attention to the scope of knowledge and not only to the objects of knowledge, to transcendence and not only to what is understood categorically in time and space within this transcendence, only then," Rahner concludes, "is one just on the threshold of becoming a religious person."[133]

NOTES

[1] Donceel notes that Maréchal's *Cahier III* was one of the first fair evaluations of the philosophy of Kant ever published by a Catholic author" (J. Maréchal, *A Maréchal Reader*, edited and translated by Joseph Donceel [New York: Herder and Herder, 1970], x). On Maréchal's influence on the thinking of Karl Rahner, see K. Rahner, *Spirit in the World*, translated by William Dych, S.J. (New York: Herder and Herder, 1967), xxi–xxii, xxxiii–xxxv, xxxvii, 18,n1; Thomas Sheehan, *Karl Rahner: The Philosophical Foundations* (Athens, Ohio: Ohio University Press, 1987), 55–102; Gerald A. McCool, "The Philosophy of the Human Person in Karl Rahner's Theology," *Theological Studies* XXII (1961): 537–539; L. M. Regis, *Epistemology* (New York: The Macmillan Company), 93–103; Georges Van Riet, *Thomistic Epistemology* (St. Louis and London: B. Herder Book Co, 1963), 236–271. Concerning Maréchal's influence on Lonergan, see Bernard J. F. Lonergan, A *Second Collection*, ed. by William F. J. Ryan, and Bernard J. Tyrrell, S. J. (London: Darton, Longman and Todd, 1974), 265; B. Lonergan, *Philosophy of God, and Theology* (Philadelphia, The Westminster Press, 1973), 62; George S. Worgul, "The Ghost of Newman in the Lonergan Corpus," *The Modern Schoolman* LIV(May, 1977), 317–318; John F. X. Knasas, "Intellectual Dynamism in Transcendental Thomism: A Metaphysical Assessment," *American Catholic Philosophical Quarterly*, LXIX, No. 1(1995), 15.

[2] For brief introductions, see Frederick Copleston, *A History of Philosophy*, Volume 2, *Mediaeval Philosophy*, II (Garden City, NY: Doubleday and Company, Inc., 1962), 109–10; F. Copleston, *Kant*, 30–32.

[3] Bernard Lonergan, *Understanding and Being* (New York and Toronto: The Edwin Mellen Press, 1980), 229.

[4] Karl Rahner, *Foundations of Christian Faith*, translated by William V. Dych (New York: The Seabury Press, 1978), 17.

[5] *Ibid.*

[6] See I. Kant, *Critique of Pure Reason*, in *GB* 42:5; and in general, for the following remarks on Kant: Copleston, *Kant*, 8–29.

[7] B. Lonergan, *Collection*, ed. by F. E. Crowe, S. J. (New York: Herder and Herder, 1967), 207–209; Giovanni Sala, "The *A Priori* in Human Knowledge: Kant's *Critique of Pure Reason* and Lonergan's *Insight*," *The Thomist* XL (April, 1976), No. 2: 179–221.

[8] Patricia Wilson, "Human Knowledge of God's Existence in the Theology of Bernard Lonergan," *The Thomist* XXXV, No. 2 (April, 1971): 260.

[9] See Copleston, *Kant*, 76, 94, 142.

[10] See the "Introduction" by Gerald A. McCool to *A Rahner Reader* (New York: The Seabury Press, 1975), xiv.

[11] Ibid.

[12] *Ibid.*, xv.

[13] See *Ibid.*, and Verkamp, *Senses of Mystery*, 114–115.

[14] McCool, "Introduction," *Rahner Reader*, xv.

[15] Lonergan, *Collection* I, 203. Lonergan himself, it may be noted, undertook this task within the context of his study of "insight," by which understanding grasps the diverse manifold of sensible data "as cohering in an orderly and intelligible whole" (see Bernard J. F. Lonergan, *Insight, A Study of Human Understanding* [London, New York, Toronto: Longmans, Green and Co., 1958], 3–12, 319–347; Hugo A. Meynell, *An Introduction to the Philosophy of Bernard Lonergan* [Toronto and Buffalo: University of Toronto Press, 1991], 2–5).

[16] See *Supra*, Chapter One, 1–2.

[17] See *Ibid.,* and *NCE* 3:981–82.

[18] Rahner, *Spirit*, 269, 278, 301; As the soul "unfolds" toward its own "fulfillment/perfection," Rahner notes further, the "power" of sensibility "flows" forth under the "unconscious guidance and inspiration of the intellect, in much the same manner as the parts of an organism (as opposed to a machine) are influenced by the whole (*Ibid.*, 256, 257, 259). Just as the soul is the substantial form of the body, so, it is said, the intellect, as an "active" principle of being, is the "form" of the senses; it "animates" them, "empowering" them, so to speak, "to meditate" or "cogitate," and thereby giving rise, in the "receptive" or "passive" intellect, to the "cogitative power" (*Ibid.*, 255, 268–279, 299–308; Donceel, *Philosophical Anthropology*, 297, 303–305, 345–346; *NCE* 3: 981–982; 7:556; 13:92).

[19] Rahner, *Spirit*, 270.

[20] *Ibid.*, 270, 271.

[21] *Ibid.*, 265, 266, 278.

[22] *Ibid.*, 271, 272, 273.

[23] *Ibid.*, 271, 273, 278.

[24] *Ibid.*, 273.

[25] *Ibid.*, 308.

[26] See Donceel, *Philosophical Anthropology*, 304, 347, 361; *NCE* 7:556; George A. Lindbeck, "The *A Priori* in St. Thomas' Theory of Knowledge," in R. E. Cushman and E. Grislis, eds., *The Heritage of Christian Thought* (New York: Harper and Row, 1965), 54.

[27] See Donceel, *Philosophical Anthropology*, 304, 348; *NCE* 7:556; 8:230.

[28] See *Great Ideas*: *GB* 2:127; Lindbeck, "*A Priori*," 57, 63.

[29] Rahner, *Spirit*, 266.

[30] *Ibid.*, 266–268.

[31] *Ibid.*, 278.

[32] *Ibid.*

[33] Donceel, *Philosophical Anthropology*, 348.

[34] *NCE* 8:230; Donceel, *Philosophical Anthropology*, 332.

[35] Rahner, *Foundations*, 17–18.

[36] *NCE* 8:231; Donceel, *Philosophical Anthropology*, 362.

[37] In Thomas' view, as interpreted by Rahner, the human soul is not a "being" or "real and complete thing with one nature and one existence"; it does not "exist for its own sake" (K. Rahner and H. Vorgrimler, *Theological Dictionary* [New York: Herder and Herder, 1965], 442). It is rather a "principle of being" in the sense that it is the "intrinsic source" from which the plurality of an entity's "powers" originate (*Ibid.*; Rahner, *Spirit*, 256–257). As the principle of spatial-temporal being, it (the human soul) "cannot fulfill itself without making use of matter" (Rahner and Vorgrimler, *Dictionary*, 60, 443). But "matter" is there "for the sake of form," (not vice versa), and under the soul's influence, is "actualized" to become a "body" which serves as "the substantial 'expression' of the soul in which the soul achieves its concrete reality" (*Ibid.*, 60, 443; Rahner, *Spirit*, 250). "The more man becomes spirit," therefore, "the more the soul becomes the body" (Rahner and Vorgrimler, *Dictionary*, 60), or, in other words, a spirit that "fulfills itself in a bodily world" (*Ibid.*). This is all the more so, Rahner contends, in view of the fact that one of the principal "powers" emanating from the soul of man is the "intellect." Were man's intellect perfect, like God's, or "quasi-perfect," like that of the angels, it would already be "perfectly (or quasi-perfectly) present to itself," and have no need of sensibility. God, in Thomas' view, "does not need an object in order to reach self-awareness" (Donceel, *Philosophical Anthropology*, 29). God's being is "self-luminous" precisely because it is not clouded by "matter," or diffused in the "pure potency" ("pure multiplicity without unity, pure indefiniteness, pure indeterminacy") of "prime matter" (*NCE* 8: 231; Donceel, *Philosophical Anthropology*, 36; Rahner, *Spirit*, 74). Material creature that he is, however, man's being is not self-luminous. Constantly on the move between the potentiality and actuality of his being, man, the knowing subject, is always, to some extent, absent to himself (Rahner, Spirit, 259; Sheehan, *Philosophical Foundations*, 195, 226, 235). But "if the [human] spirit of itself alone has not already and always consciously possessed itself or another, then it is immediately evident," Rahner writes, that it "must receive knowledge from external things," from "an object different from the knower" (*Spirit*, 252; *NCE* 8:232). For that to happen, the object known must become "intentionally present in the knowing subject," while at the same time being recognized as "existing outside the subject and as distinct from it" (*NCE* 8:231). The human intellect will be able to "intend" its object in such wise, however, only if it has some "sensibility" (Rahner, *Spirit*, 252–259; Donceel, *Philosophical Anthropology*, 294, 295, 345–346).

[38] Rahner, *Spirit*, 259. Not only things like cars and trees that are external to himself, but even his own body, his own emotions, drives, and thoughts, Donceel notes, do not perfectly "coincide" with him as a knowing subject; they always remain to some extent something the knowing subject "has," as opposed to "being" (Donceel, *Philosophical Anthropology*, 24–27).

[39] Rahner, *Foundations*, 20, 21, 33; Rahner, *Spirit*, 142–145, 205.

[40] See especially, Rahner, *Foundations*, 20–21.

[41] *Ibid.*, 20.

[42] *Ibid.*

[43] *Ibid.*, 19, 33, 58, 62, 64, 69.

[44] The "abstractive power of the cogitative sense might be said to be like a great searchlight (see Rahner, *Spirit*, 211–216; Donceel, *Philosophical Anthropology*, 34, 209, 305); as soon as an object "crosses its beam," it is immediately judged to be "something"—an "instance" or "limited determination" of the infinite fullness of Being (Donceel, *Philosophical Anthropology*, 332, 349; *NCE* 7:556). It is not that the knowing subject affirms it to be a being because it knows that it is a being, but the other way around: it knows that it is a being, because it affirms it (Donceel, *Philosophical Anthropology*, 332). This universal concept which constitutes man's "first intellectual contact with reality" (*NCE* 8:231), therefore, is an "affirmed concept," a "concept embedded in a judgment," and this judgment serves, in Rahner's interpretation of Thomas, as a sort of "substitute for the intuition of pure spirits" (*NCE* 7:556; Donceel, *Philosophical Anthropology*, 362). As the knowing subject makes such a judgment, affirming the being of the object encountered, there is a concomitant, simultaneous, immediate, and direct, albeit imperfect, "intuition" of the knowing subject's "originating I" as a being who has a natural and insatiable desire to know "in a more perfect manner" not only this one, particular, finite, and limited entity, but "many more beings," and ultimately, the "unlimited infinite totality of all being" (Donceel, *Philosophical Anthropology*, 33, 35, 358, 362; Rahner, *Foundations*, 17–19, 20–21; Rahner, *Spirit*, 145; *NCE* 8:232). The object is experienced as "limited," and therefore as incapable of satisfying man's quest for the "unlimited" (Donceel, *Philosophical Anthropology*, 358). It is recognized as an "end," but only as an "intermediate end," one that refers the knowing subject beyond itself to "something more" (*Ibid.*, 358, 362). As the intellect affirms the "being" of the object, it also subsumes the object under the "laws of being," or, in other words, the so-called "First Principles," and thereby brings into focus its relation to "Self-Existent Being" and to "that which is intelligible in itself" (see Rahner, *Spirit*, 202–211; Donceel, *Philosophical Anthropology*, 332, 358–359, 362; Lindbeck, "*A Priori*," 53–56).

[45] See: Rahner, *Foundations*, 21; Lonergan, *Understanding and Being*, 201; and Emerich Coreth, *Metaphysics* (New York: Herder and Herder, 1968), 46–54.

[46] Rahner, *Foundations*, 32.

[47] *Ibid.*; Coreth, *Metaphysics*, 105–109.

[48] Rahner, *Foundations*, 32.

[49] Lonergan, *Insight*, 9, 172, 185, 330, 348, 356; *Collection* I, 204.

[50] Lonergan, *Collection* I, 204; "Basic propositions are counter-positions," Lonergan notes, "if they are expressions which are contradictory to the expressions of intelligent and rational consciousness as orientated to the universe of being" (*Understanding and Being*, 229). It is part of a "retorsive" method whereby an assertion is demonstrated "by showing that he who denies the assertion affirms it in his very denial" (J. Donceel, "Transcendental Thomism," *The Monist* 58 (1974): 81; Knasas, "Intellectual Dynamism," 23,n29).

[51] Rahner, *Foundations*, 48; Rahner, *Spirit*, 57–64; Lonergan, *Understanding and Being*, 46–50; Coreth, *Metaphysics*, 46–50.

[52] Lonergan, *Collection*, I, 205.

[53] *Ibid.*

[54] Rahner, *Foundations*, 20.

[55] *Ibid.*

[56] *Ibid.*

[57] K. Rahner, *Christian at the Crossroads* (New York: The Seabury Press, 1975), 11, 15; K. Rahner, "The Concept of Mystery in Catholic Theology," in K. Rahner, *Theological Investigations* IV (London: Darton, Longman, and Todd, 1966), 54–55.

[58] Lonergan, *Understanding and Being*, 327. Like Plato, who had compared the Idea of the Good with the sun, in the sense that the Idea of the Good "irradiates the subordinate intelligible objects of Ideas" (Plato, *Republic*, 509: *GB* 7: 386), Augustine, it may be noted in passing, embraced the light-metaphor, and combining it with Plotinus' identification of the Platonic ideas with the "thoughts of God," came to the conclusion that God is the "intelligible light" which "performs the same function for the objects of the mind as the sun's light performs for the objects of the eye (Copleston, *Mediaeval Philosophy*, I: 75–78; *NCE* 7:367). What exactly Augustine meant by all this is a matter of considerable debate. According to Copleston, Augustine certainly did not mean to suggest that humans somehow enjoy direct intuition into the mind of God, or that the human mind is infused by God with the actual ideas (*Mediaeval Philosophy*, I: 78, 79, 80, 82). But it would also be wrong, Copleston adds, "to reduce the illumination-theory to nothing more than a statement of the truth that God conserves and creates the human intellect and that the natural light of the intellect is a participated light" (*Ibid.*, 78–79). At the very least, it is Augustine's view, Copleston concludes, that "a special illuminative action of God, beyond His creative and conserving activity," is necessary, if the contingent and changeable human mind is ever to discover what is genuinely intelligible in a world of ever-changing sensible objects; the human mind must be enabled by the "regulative influence of the divine ideas . . . to see the relation of created things to eternal supersensible realities . . . and to discern the elements of necessity, immutability, and eternity" in any judgment about reality (*Ibid.*, 81–82). To that extent, Copleston adds, "divine illumination takes the place in Augustine's thought of reminiscence in the Platonic philosophy" (*Ibid.*, 80, 81). While some medieval thinkers, like Bonaventure, would continue to invoke Augustine's theory of illumination (*Ibid.*, 316–19), and although Thomas himself would continue to talk about "divine ideas" in the sense of "objective (as opposed to formal) concepts" or "objects known" (*NCE* 7:338), the latter would deny the necessity of any special divine illumination (see Thomas Aquinas, *Summa Theologica*, I, 79, 3: *GB* 19: 416; I, 84, 6: *GB* 19: 448; I, 85, 1 and 2: *GB* 19: 451–455; Copleston, *Mediaeval Philosophy*, I: 79, 81), and by way of "retrieving" the Aristotelian theories of hylomorphism and abstraction, insist upon the human mind's own ability to discern the intelligible in the sensible.

[59] Lonergan, *Insight*, 636.

[60] Rahner, *Foundations*, 32.

[61] Ibid. See also Anne Carr's discussion of this point: A. Carr, "Starting with the Human," in *A World of Grace*, ed. Leo J. O'Donovan (New York: Crossroad, 1989), 19–20.

[62] Lonergan, *Collection* II, 124.

[63] Rahner, *Foundations*, 33–34.

[64] *Ibid.*, 33, 34, 58.

[65] *Ibid.*, 60; also *Ibid.*, 20, 33; Lonergan, *Insight*, 348–374.

[66] Rahner, *Foundations*, 60.

[67] The "mystery" that is the term of human transcendence must also be designated as "holy," Rahner states, so as to emphasize that "when we speak of transcendence we do not mean only and exclusively the transcendence which is the condition of possibility for categorical knowledge as such. We mean also and just as much the *transcendence of freedom, of willing, and of love*"(*Ibid.*, 65).

[68] *Ibid.*, 21, 60, 65.

[69] *Ibid.*, 61–65.

[70] *Ibid.*, 21.

[71] *Ibid.*, 60, 61.

[72] *Ibid.*, 46.

[73] *Ibid.*, 61; see also: Rahner, *Crossroads*, 32, 33, 17.

[74] K. Rahner, "Priest and Poet," in *The Word: Readings in Theology*, ed. Carney Gavin, Charles Pfeiffer, et al. (New York: P. J. Kenedy, and Sons, 1964), 4–5.

[75] *Ibid.*, 6, 7.

[76] Rahner, *Foundations*, 21, 51–55.

[77] *Ibid.*, 52.

[78] *Ibid.*, 52, 64, 65, 67; see also the entry on "ontologism" in *NCE* 10:701–703.

[79] Rahner, *Foundations*, 64–65.

[80] *Ibid.*, 53.

[81] *Ibid.*, 52, 53.

[82] *Ibid.*, 33, 58, 62, 64, 69.

[83] *Ibid.*, 18, 19.

[84] *Ibid.*, 18–19, 35, 52–53, 68.

[85] *Ibid.*, 21; also: *Ibid.*, 18, 53, 58, 69.

[86] *Ibid.*, 18.

[87] See Lindbeck, "*A Priori*," 43–44; Francis P. Fiorenza's introduction to Rahner's *Spirit* (xliii–xliv); Karl-Heinz Weger, *Karl Rahner: An Introduction to His Theology* (New York: Seabury Press, 1980), 47–50.

[88] Rahner, *Foundations*, 54.

[89] *Ibid.*, 61.

[90] *Ibid.*, 54.

[91] *Ibid.*, 61, 63.

[92] *Ibid.*, 54.

[93] *Ibid.*, 61–62.

[94] *Ibid.*, 54.

[95] *Ibid.*, 62, 66.

[96] *Ibid.*, 21.

[97] *Ibid.*, 66–67.

[98] *Ibid.*, 67.

[99] *Ibid.*, 34.

[100] *Ibid.*, 65.

[101] *Ibid.*, 58.

[102] *Ibid.*, 59.

[103] *Ibid.*, 58, 65–66.

[104] *Ibid.*, 64.

[105] *Ibid.*, 57, 34.

[106] See: Bernard J. F. Lonergan, *Method in Theology* (Toronto: University of Toronto Press, 1990), 105, 111; see also: Eugene Webb, *Philosophers of Consciousness* (Seattle and London: University of Washington Press, 1988), 70–72; William E. Reiser, "Lonergan's Notion of the Religious *Apriori*," *The Thomist* XXXV, 2 (April, 1971): 247–258.

[107] Lonergan, *Method*, 111, 23–24.

[108] Lonergan, *Understanding and Being*, 303; *Collection*, II, 40–42.

[109] Lonergan, *Collection*, II, 40, 123.

110 *Ibid.*, 123.
111 *Ibid.*, 40.
112 *Ibid.*
113 *Ibid.*, 41.
114 *Ibid.*, 41–42.
115 *Ibid.*
116 *Ibid.*, 123.
117 *Ibid.*, 41.
118 *Ibid.*, 123.
119 *Ibid.*, 124; Lonergan, *Insight*, 683; Reiser, "Religious *Apriori*," 256.
120 Lonergan, *Understanding and Being*, 203.
121 Rahner, *Foundations*, 32–33; Rahner, *Crossroads*, 15.
122 Rahner, *Crossroads*, 12.
123 Rahner, *Foundations*, 33.
124 *Ibid.*, 48–49.
125 *Ibid.*, 68–70.
126 *Ibid.*, 68, 69.
127 *Ibid.*, 68.
128 Rahner, *Crossroads*, 15.
129 Rahner, *Foundations*, 21.
130 *Ibid.*, 22.
131 Lonergan, *Method*, 103.
132 *Ibid.*
133 Rahner, *Foundations*, 23.

CHAPTER FIVE

Primary Apprehension/ Mystical Perception

Like the term experience itself,[1] the expression religious experience admits of a variety of definitions and applications. In the discussion of numinous and transcendental experiences by the likes of Schleiermacher, Fries, and Otto, or by Rahner and Lonergan, for example, we have already seen in previous chapters, how religious experience can be used to designate a dimension or aspect of all experience.[2] But more often than not religious experience is thought to refer to one or another unique event through which an individual lives with an awareness of an encounter with God (or some other mysterious entity or Ultimate Reality).[3] William P. Alston, for example, will describe as religious "only those experiences in which it seems that God 'appears' or 'presents Himself' to one as so-and-so."[4] As Richard Swinburne and others have noted, however, there are many different ways of encountering God.[5] And Alston himself identifies three basically different "grades of immediacy" in which the object of religious experience (i.e., God, Mystery, etc). can "present" itself to the religious person.[6] In the remainder of this chapter, we will be following Alston's distinctions in this regard so as to clarify not only his own "perceptualist" interpretation of the religious sense of mystery, but also ways of explaining the latter in "experiential" terms other than those already discussed in previous chapters.

At one level, according to Alston, is a "grade of immediacy," in which "one is aware of X [God/Mystery] through the awareness of another object of perception."[7] He calls this grade "mediate perception."[8] The experience by primitive peoples of "hierophanies" in nature, as identified by Otto, Eliade, and others in a previous chapter,[9] might conceivably be included in this category of "indirect perception" of God.[10] More obvious examples of such indirect perception of God abound in contemporary philosophical and theological literature, where, as Alston observes, one finds so much "talk of experiencing God in the beauties of nature, of hearing God's voice in the Bible, or in sermons or in the dictates of conscience, of being aware of God's providential activity in the events of our lives, of seeing God's hand at work in salvation history, and so on."[11] Typical in this regard were the 1962 Gifford Lectures delivered by John Baillie.

Entitled *The Sense of the Presence of God*, Baillie tried in his lectures to explain "faith" as a "primary apprehension" or a "primary mode of awareness."[12] He starts with a consideration of the possibility of God being perceived by the senses as a "phenomenon." Due to the tendency of the early Hebrews to conceive of God as having a body,[13] the Old Testament (e.g., Exodus), Baillie noted, could speak of a human being like Moses as having seen, if not the face, at least the "back parts" of God (Exodus 33:17–33).[14] But by New Testament times, he adds, it had come to be taken for granted that God is "incorporeal," and that "no man has seen God at any time" (John 1:18).[15] The New Testament writers, however, had never allowed this latter assertion to stand "unqualified."[16] Although they dismiss the possibility of seeing God with the "bodily eyes," they did nonetheless speak of a perception of God with the "eyes of faith."[17] If, therefore, the word see is used in its primary sense of seeing with the eyes of flesh,[18] it may very well be, Baillie noted, that "no man has seen God at any time since God is not a corporeal being located in space."[19] But the word see can also be used, he continued, "in its derivative and no doubt symbolic sense of seeing with what we may call the eyes of the spirit, or, if you prefer it, the eyes of the mind."[20]

Baillie acknowledged in his aforementioned Gifford Lectures that most contemporary philosophers recognize only the external senses as being capable of delivering knowledge of trans-subjective reality. But it was his own view that humans have "even what can properly be called *sense* experience" of things other than "what we can see and hear and touch and taste and smell."[21] "For, the human spirit," he said, "develops certain subtler senses or sensitivities which go beyond the bodily senses."[22] They are "refined or sublimate developments of our experience," and although they "presuppose . . . the experience gained through the bodily senses," they transcend such experience, and make us "sensitive to aspects of reality of which [the bodily senses], taken by themselves, could not conceivably inform us."[23] "They enable us to perceive ['and not merely to conceive'] something not otherwise perceptible," and to that extent are "analogous to the corporeal senses."[24] Citing Cardinal Newman's discussion of the "illative sense," Baillie noted how, as Newman also had observed, we often speak of a sense of beauty, a sense of humor, a sense of duty, and so forth.[25] Other examples can be found, he said, in John Locke's suggestion that "though [introspection] is not sense, yet it is very like it,"[26] or in the contention of contemporary philosophers such as G. E. Moore, David Ross, and H. A. Pritchard, to the effect that "in the exercise of our moral consciousness we are being aware, in a way that is analogous to sense-perception, of aspects or properties of reality other than those of which we are aware in sense-perception itself."[27] According to P. H. Nowell-Smith's interpretation of the latter, "we do not literally see these properties with our eyes; but the faculty concerned is called 'non-sensuous intuition,' 'awareness,' 'apprehension,' 'recognition,' 'acquaintance,' words which all strongly suggest an analogy with sight or touch."[28] And among such "subtler senses or sensitivities which go beyond the bodily sense," Baillie concluded, is to be counted especially "a sense of the holy or of the divine, a sense of the presence of God."[29]

The vision resulting from this "inner sense of the presence of God" is what Baillie means by seeing with the "eyes of faith." Faith, he concludes, is "a mode of experience,"[30] or "a mode of primary apprehension . . . which perceives something more in the total reality with which we are confronted than is manifest, or is expected to be manifest, to the [external] senses."[31] In the context of "familiar experience," such as the Incarnation, an encounter with a neighbor, or natural, historical, or societal events, the "eyes of faith" can "perceive" the presence of God.[32]

In making such a claim for the "mediated perception" of God, Baillie, it should be emphasized, was referring to "an awareness of the divine Presence itself, however hidden behind the veils of sense," and was not, therefore, talking about any attempt "to deduce from other realities that *are* present the existence of a God who is *not* present but absent."[33] "My main contention throughout," Baillie concluded at the end of his lectures, "has been that we have to do, not with an absent God about whom we have a certain amount of information, but with a

God whose living and active presence with us can be perceived by faith in a large variety of human contexts and situations."[34]

As Baillie himself acknowledged, his conclusions in this regard are very much in line with those of John Hick. Like Baillie, Hick will define "faith" as "a mode of putative awareness of the divine."[35] Quoting John Calvin to the effect that there is "a sense of divinity which can never be effaced engraved upon men's minds,"[36] Hick argues that it must be admitted that "man is a worshiping animal, with an ingrained propensity to construe his world religiously," or a "tendency to interpret [human] experience in religious terms,"[37] or, in still other words, "a tendency to experience [man's environment] 'in depth,' as a supernatural as well as a natural environment," or as "other and greater than it seems."[38] But the reality experienced by man is not unambiguous. In order to preserve man's cognitive freedom in relation to God, God remains for a man a "*deus absconditus*,"[39] or a God, in other words, who "stand[s] back, hiding himself behind his creation, and leaving to us the freedom to recognize or fail to recognize his dealings with us."[40] Just as "there is in cognition of every kind an unresolved mystery," so too, Hick says, in "the apprehension of God": "The theistic believer cannot explain *how* he knows the divine presence to be mediated through his human experience. He just finds himself interpreting his experience in this way. He lives in the presence of God, though he is unable to prove by any dialectical process that God exists."[41]

Faith, then, according to Hick, is the actualization of this innate tendency to interpret reality religiously. He writes that "we become conscious of the existence of other objects in the universe, whether things or persons, either by experiencing them for ourselves or by inferring their existence from evidences within our experience."[42] "The awareness of God reported by the ordinary religious believer is of the former kind," Hick concludes, for "he professes, not to have inferred that there is a God, but that God as a living being has entered into his own experience."[43] According to Hick, therefore, "faith is not to be described as either a reasoned conclusion or an unreasoned hunch that there is a God. It is, putatively, an apprehension of the divine presence within the believer's human experience. It is not an inference to a general truth, but a 'divine-human encounter,' a mediated meeting with the living God."[44] It is a meeting of God, in other words, not "as existing in isolation from all other objects of experience," but "in and through his material and social environment."[45]

The "basic epistemological pattern" of this "mediated knowledge [awareness], such as is postulated by [the] religious claim,"[46] Hick goes on to say, "is that of all our knowing," namely, "a primary and unevidenceable act of interpretation" of "significance" or "meaning."[47] "The discovery of God as lying behind the world, and of his presence as mediated in and through it," therefore, "is epistemologically comparable," he notes, "to what Wittgenstein called 'seeing as,'" except that "we must expand the notion of 'seeing as' into that of 'experiencing as,' not only visually but through all the modes of perception functioning together."[48] As an example, Hick cites the case of the Old Testament prophets "experiencing" the same ancient Jewish history, which secular historians interpret as nothing more than the interplay of various economic, social, and geographical factors, "as one in which they were living under the sovereign claim of God."[49] Another example, he notes, can be found in the New Testament account of how Jesus, encountered by non-believers as just another human being, was "experienced" by his disciples "as a prophet," or "as mediating the transforming presence of God."[50]

Hick, it should be noted further, consistently distinguished this type of "mediated" religious experience from what he defines as a "mystical" religious experience, in which "instead of being mediated through the outer world of nature and history," the "impact of a transcendent reality . . . is directly prehended at some deep level of the mystic's psyche and then expressed in forms supplied by his or her mind."[51] But common to the whole spectrum of religious experience, he insists, is the "epistemological character" of being "joint products of the impact of a transcendent reality" and the religious person's "own mind set."[52] What this implies, of course, is that the religious experience is like any other interpretative activity to the extent of "always imply[ing] concepts."[53] What makes the religious experience unique is that in the process of interpreting the mediated object the religious person employs "distinctively religious concepts."[54]

This latter point is essential to Hick's understanding of religious pluralism.[55] In Alston's view, however, it only serves to compromise Hick's claim for "immediacy" in the religious experience. While admitting that "normal, adult sense perception, and spiritual perception as well, is heavily conceptualized," or that "normal perceptual experience is shot through with 'interpretation,'" Alston argues that the direct awareness afforded by the presentation of the object in perception "is something that is distinguishable from any elements of conceptualization, judgment, belief, or other forms of 'interpretation,' however rarely the former may be found without the latter in adult experience."[56] "Any sort of interpretation," therefore, "is something over and above" the "direct awareness" that comes with the "presentation" of the object.[57] By involving all experience in conceptualized interpretation, therefore, Hick, according to Alston, is in fact jeopardizing the element of immediacy in the religious experience, for although, like Baillie, he will talk of a "mediate perception," what he is really saying, Alston argues, "sounds like what I termed 'indirect perceptual recognition,'"[58] wherein one takes something "as a sign or indication of X but does not see X itself . . . as when I take a vapor trail across the sky as an indication that a jet plane has flown by . . . [but] I don't see the plane at all."[59]

Notwithstanding these objections to Hick's insistence upon the role of conceptualization in the religious interpretation of reality, Alston has, it should be noted, overcome his original skepticism about the possibility of any indirect perception of the divine presence ever actually occurring. At the prompting of students in some of his graduate seminars, he eventually came to drop his objections to this possibility, and now admits that "if God can appear to me as loving or powerful or glorious when I am not sensorially aware of a field of oats or the words of the Bible," there is no reason "why He shouldn't also appear to me as loving or powerful or glorious when that comes through my sense perception of the field of oats or whatever."[60]

While acknowledging the possibility of such "indirect perception" of the object of religious experience, Alston's own explanation of the "perceptual" nature of the religious sense focuses more on the second "grade of immediacy," which he calls "mediated immediacy," and wherein "one is aware of X [God/Mystery] through a state of consciousness that is distinguishable from X, and can be made an object of absolutely immediate awareness, but is not perceived."[61] To illustrate what he means thereby, Alston cites multiple samples of first hand accounts of personal "mystical" experiences provided by thousands of Englanders in response to a request made in 1969 by Professor Sir Alister Hardy, the founder and first director of Oxford's Religious Experience Research Unit, and reported by Timothy Beardsworth in a book entitled *A Sense of Presence*.[62] What qualifies these samples as "cases of Mediated Immediacy rather than Mediated Perception," Alston notes, "is that while speaking of a direct awareness or presentation of God, they do not mention any other presented or perceived object, in or through which they are aware of God."[63] But they do involve "a specifiable mode of consciousness through which God is perceived," and which is recognized as being distinct from the object (God) perceived.[64] To that extent, such experiences are also to be differentiated from cases of what Alston calls "extreme mystical experience" which, as we will see later in this chapter, belong to a third "grade of immediacy" referred to by Alston as "absolute immediacy."[65] In analyzing these cases of "mediated immediacy," Alston has no intention of trying to prove that the object of religious experience actually exists.[66] His primary concern is rather to investigate the extent to which the putative *perception* of God can contribute to the grounds of religious belief.[67] Toward that end he first uses the aforementioned samples of "mediated immediacy" to demonstrate the possibility and meaning of a "perception" of God. It is only with this latter aspect of his discussion that we will be concerned here.

From a strictly empirical perspective, "perception" is usually defined as the synthetic observation of all the sensations (colors, sounds, odors, etc.) provided by the five external senses of sight, hearing, smell, touch, and taste.[68] To say, therefore, that humans can "perceive" God would seem to imply that humans might be able to experience God through use of their external senses. And Alston does not altogether rule out that possibility. While acknowledging the aforementioned biblical passage about "no man ever having seen God,"[69] he observes how it is "qualified" by the Christian doctrine of the Incarnation, according to which, "to see [Jesus], even in human form, is to see God,"[70] and is seemingly "opposed" by several other biblical passages.[71] And even if we conceive of God as not possessing, in His own nature, any sensory qualities, Alston adds, "it is not inconceivable that [He] should appear to us as looking bright or sounding a certain way."[72] For, "it is a familiar point from sense perception that the way an object phenomenally appears may not correspond exactly to the way it is," and "there is a long tradition that holds that secondary qualities like colors do not really characterize physical substances."[73] Thus, it might be not only conceivable but even "fitting" that a purely spiritual God would appear in a sensory manner. "Given our powers and proclivities," Alston notes, it might be the "best way for Him to get a certain message across; just as, even if physical substances are not really colored, the system of color appearances enables us to make many useful distinctions between them."[74] Alston also admits, however, that if God exists, our "better chance of grasping [His] purely spiritual, essential nature" is to be found in the "non-sensory" perception or experience of God.[75]

A non-sensory perception of God is not ruled out, Alston claims, by the biblical assertion that "no man has ever seen God." For even if John had had in mind to deny the possibility of a "*visual* presentation of God," or of "the kind of clear, unmistakable, chock-full-of-information sort of awareness of God that we have of physical objects when we see them without eyes," that is not to be construed, Alston notes, "as denying the possibility of a non-sensory presentation of God."[76] In any event, it is the non-sensory perception of God that Alston primarily has in mind when he talks about the sense of God's presence. What he means, in other words, is that the religious experience is analogous to, but not necessarily identical with, sense perception.[77]

In trying to establish such an analogy, Alston, it may be noted first of all, does not have much to say about any kind of "inner sense" by which humans are enabled to experience the presence of God. He does, however, cite approvingly the following quotation from the Introduction to Louis du Pont's *Meditations*, which reiterates what Baillie especially had claimed in this regard:

> As the body has its five exterior senses, with which it perceives the visible and delectable things of this life, and makes experience of them, so the spirit, with its faculties of understanding and will, has five interior acts corresponding to these senses, which we call seeing, hearing, smelling, tasting, and, touching spiritually, with which it perceives the invisible and delectable things of Almighty God, and makes *experience* of them.[78]

Alston's major emphasis, however, is upon how "mystical perception" is like sense perception in the way the object of both is "presented, given, or appears," and the subject enjoys a "direct awareness" of the object.[79] "That something *presents* itself to the subject's awareness as so-and-so as red, round, loving, or whatever," Alston notes, is "what I take to be definitive of perceptual consciousness," and "differentiates perceptual consciousness from other modes of consciousness," and especially from "abstract thought."[80] "The most fundamental fact about sense perception," he adds, "is the way in which seeing my house differs from thinking about it, remembering it, forming mental images of it, reasoning about it, and so on. It is the difference between *presence* (to consciousness) and absence. If I stand before my house with my eyes shut and then open them, I am suddenly *presented* with the object itself."[81] For the object of sense perception to be "presented" in such wise, Alston notes, it must "appear" to the subject with such sensory *qualia* as color, shape, pitch, etc.[82] In other words, the object must be a "phenomenon."[83] For mystical perception to be genuinely analogous to sense perception, therefore, it must, Alston claims, involve "presentation" of its object,[84] and for that to happen it must also "involve distinctive phenomenal content."[85]

But can there be any real "presentation" in religious perception, if, as noted earlier, such perception is assumed to be without any external, sensory content? Alston sees no reason why there cannot be. It is possible, he says, to envisage "presentations that do not stem from the activity of any physical sense organs," and "there is no reason to doubt that phenomenal content may be very different from any that is produced by our external senses and may not result from the stimulation of any physical sense organ."[86] In this regard, however, Alston readily admits how difficult it might be to actually specify "any basic phenomenal qualities for mystical perception, analogous to color and shape for the visual modality and temperature and texture for the tactile."[87] "It must be confessed," he adds, that we are quite incapable of enumerating the basic phenomenal qualities of which 'divine phenomena' are configurations."[88] The inability of individuals to enumerate these *qualia*, however, "no more prevents them from perceiving God through being aware of the *qualia* than the inability of one of us to analyze a rural scene into its constituent basic visual *qualia* prevents us from perceiving that scene."[89] "The supposition that mystical perception involves distinctive, nonaffective phenomenal *qualia*," Alston adds, can be shored up by the long-standing Catholic, mystical tradition, in which numerous accounts are to be found of God "appearing" to one or another mystic in ways analogous to the sensory *qualia* of odor, color, sound, etc., and thereby affording the mystic a "spiritual sensation."[90]

Against theorists such as Wayne Proudfoot "and his ilk," who construe all religious experiences "as purely subjective feelings or sensations to which is superadded an *explanation* according to which they are due to God, the Holy Spirit, or some other agent recognized by the theology of the subject's tradition,"[91] Alston, therefore, concludes that many of the examples of mystical perception provided by Beardsworth and others clearly imply that "something, namely, God, has been *presented* or *given* to their consciousness, in generically the same way as that in which objects in the environment are (apparently) *presented* to one's consciousness in sense perception."[92]

"What is called *presentation, givenness,* or *appearance,*" from "the side of the object," Alston goes on to note, "is called *direct awareness* . . . from the side of the subject."[93] Contrary to the assumption of nineteenth century idealists and pragmatists that "there could be no form of cognition that is not mediated by general concepts and judgment," and the "prejudice of analytical philosophers against un-analyzable concepts," Alston insists that even though "a person's conceptual scheme and beliefs can affect the way in which an object presents itself to him," sensory perception remains "a mode of cognition that is essentially independent of any conceptualization, belief, judgment, or any other application of general concepts to the object, though it typically exists in close connection with the latter."[94] And the same is true, he says, of mystical perception.[95] Challenging once again, but from a different perspective, what he calls the "interesting confusions" of Proudfoot's supposition that all religious experiences (e.g., Schleiermacher's "feeling of dependency") "really involve an *interpretation* of an essentially subjective experience,"[96] Alston contends that the awareness involved in many of the mystical experiences reported by Beardsworth and others contrasts "with thinking about God, calling up mental images, entertaining pro-positions, reasoning, engaging in overt or covert conversation, remembering."[97] It is, in other words, a "direct awareness," in which the object of the experience, namely "God," is "*immediately present*" to the person having the experience, but with an "immediacy" that is different from that found in the aforementioned "mediated perception" championed by Baillie and Hick, or from the "absolute" kind found in "extreme mystical experience."[98]

As noted earlier, it is not Alston's intention to use religious experience as a proof for God's existence. He readily admits that the perception of God he is talking about is "putative." When, therefore, he refers to the "perception of *God,*" as he does, what he means is that the person having such an experience of God's presence "takes him/herself to be aware of a being that exhibits the features deemed crucial in [the major theistic religions, but not to the total exclusion of the non-theistic traditions] for the status of divinity."[99] These, Alson notes, would include "being the source of existence of all other than itself, goodness, justice, moral law-giver, having a purpose for creation, and offering salvation to mankind."[100] Although Alston purposely excludes "ineffability" from such a list, because the subjects of mystical perception "manage to say quite a lot about their experiences and about what they take themselves to be experiencing,"[101] he also acknowledges the frequency of claims by the same subjects about the "indescribability" of their experience, and concludes that such claims can best be taken "as denials that the experience can be specified literally in terms taken from common experience, so that recourse must be had to metaphor, analogy, symbols, and so on, if one is to give a detailed account."[102]

The third "grade of immediacy" in the awareness of God's presence identified by Alston is that of "absolute immediacy," in which "one is aware of X [God/Mystery] but not through anything else, even a state of consciousness."[103] Involved here, according to Alston, is an "extreme mystical experience in which all distinctions are transcended in an undifferentiated unity."[104] And it is on that account especially that it is said to belong to a different category than the theistic type of mystical experience favored by Alston himself, in which an "object" (i.e., the personal God) is presented to the experiencing "subject."[105]

There are, of course, multiple reports from theistic mystics of experiences of undifferentiated unity.[106] The sixteenth century German mystic Jakob Boehme, for example, identified a certain way of knowing in which "the subjective-objective distinction has been transcended."[107] He labeled this intuitive way of knowing *Verstand*, so as to distinguish it from the more "conceptual" way of thinking, which he called *Vernunft*, and which supposedly comprehends nothing of the divine reality but the "husk."[108] In this regard, it may be noted that Evelyn Underhill, Ninian Smart, John Hick, and other scholars, even while acknowledging the difference between the immediate mystical experience and its various interpretations, nonetheless tend to think that all mystical experiences are basically the same, and on that account are generally inclined to conclude that the theistic experience is actually an "incomplete nondual one."[109] But Alston, without entering the debate about the "superiority" of nondual over dual mystical experiences,[110] argues that "when a theistic mystic who supposes God to be an objective reality reports an experience of an undifferentiated unity, she is best construed not as denying the existence of any real distinctions, for example, between herself and God, but as simply reporting that she is aware of no such distinctions, or of any other, at that time."[111] According to Alston, therefore, the theistic mystical experience is not really of a nondual nature, and for genuine examples of the latter we have to turn to one or another of the nontheistic religious traditions. No better example could be found, perhaps, than in Mahayana Buddhism and its notion of *prajna*.

The term *prajna* derives from *pra*, meaning "being born or springing up," and *jna*, meaning "knowing" or "knowledge."[112] And, as we shall see, this has always been considered one important dimension of *prajna*. The prefix *"pra,"* however, has also been interpreted sometimes to mean "super,"[113] thus bringing into better focus the traditional definition of *prajna* as "transcendental wisdom," or the kind of "knowledge" that comes with having "gone beyond."[114] In one of the shortest but most important of the Mahayana sutras,[115] the so-called *Heart Sutra*, for example, the "awakened mind" is said to have "gone, gone, gone beyond, gone completely beyond."[116] Another word in the Mahayana tradition for such wisdom is *bodhi*,[117] which ever since Siddartha Guatama's "realization" under the *Bodhi*-tree has been used to connote "enlightenment."[118] *Prajna*, therefore, is the kind of knowledge possessed by the "enlightened one," namely "the Buddha," or by anyone who has "awaken[ed] to one's own buddha-nature."[119] In the Japanese Zen branch of Mahayana Buddhism, such an "attainment of Buddhahood" is popularly referred to as *"sartori,"* literally, "insight."[120]

In trying to elucidate the meaning of *prajna*, the preeminent Zen scholar, D.T. Suzuki, often contrasts it with another kind of knowing called *vijnana*.[121] By *vijnana*, he says, is meant, "reason or discursive understanding."[122] It is "the principle of bifurcation and conceptualization,"[123] "the principle of differentiation,"[124] always "busy[ing] itself with parts."[125] It is "methodological,"[126] "analytical,"[127] "abstract,"[128] "deliberative,"[129] "divisive,"[130] and "wordy."[131] *Vijnana*, it should be noted, is said to rely on the unitive vision of *prajna* to be able to operate as the principle of differentiation,[132] and can be "recalled to its proper and original office whereby it can work in harmony with *prajna*."[133] But on its own, Suzuki notes, *vijnana* "works for individualization and, by making each individual disconnected with others, [it] makes them all impermanent and subject to the law of *karma*,"[134] and trapping them in the world of *samsara*, the vicious cycle of rebirth.[135] It conjures up, in other words, "a world of beings and non-beings," a world of clear cut definitions,"[136] a dualistic world, in which "there is one who sees and there is the other that is seen—the two standing in opposition."[137]

Prajna, on the other hand, is said to be "intuitive."[138] It is "like perception" to the extent that "it always demands immediacy."[139] It affords "no intervening moment for reflection or analysis or interpretation," no room for "deliberation" or "intervening propositions" or passage "from premises to conclusion."[140] Because of this emphasis upon the need for quickness, *prajna* is often likened "to a flash of lightning,"[141] and bears some resemblance to the "sudden means of escape" that one finds in the solution of a difficult problem and exclaims "Eureka!, Eureka!"[142] But *prajna*, Suzuki and others insist, is "a very special form of intuition," and it would be a mistake to identify it with "ordinary intuition," or with "the kind of intuition we have generally in philosophical and religious discourses."[143] "Perception," for example, is also "a form of intuition."[144] But for Kant and many others, albeit not for Alston, perception is usually restricted to "sensory intuition." And with the latter, it is said, *prajna* "has nothing in common,"[145] except for the aforementioned "immediacy" of the act. "The difference between the two," Suzuki observes, "is that perception does not go beyond the senses whereas intuition [*prajna*] is far more deeply seated."[146] In sensible intuition, for example, a flower that is seen is immediately known to be a flower, "but when *prajna* takes the flower, it wants us to take not only the flower but at the same time what is not the flower, in other words, to see the flower before it came into existence."[147] This is not to say that perception cannot become "enlightened." Suzuki notes that perception can "develop into *prajna*" when it has added to it from within the act of "*prajna* intuiting itself."[148] But on its own, sensible intuition is in a different class than *prajna*.[149]

In his study of Nagarjuna's Madhyamika system of Mahayana Buddhism, T. R. V. Murti elaborates further on this difference. As "a specific empirical act," sensory intuition, he says, is "a transitory act with a limited content," whereas "*prajna* is not a transitory state, being the very nature of all things."[150] Nor, he adds, can *prajna* be thought of as "a special faculty with a limited scope."[151] Suzuki, it may be noted, does on occasion refer to *prajna* as a "higher faculty."[152] In doing so, however, he does not have in mind to contradict Murti. In fact, he repeatedly denies that *prajna* is a special faculty. "To think that there is a special faculty called *prajna*," he states at one point, would be to "make *prajna* an aspect of *vijnana*," which it is not.[153] For, as Murti puts it, *prajna* "is not a special faculty depending on causes and conditions; it is the intellect freed of conceptual restrictions by the negative function of the dialectic; it is the *prius* of all functions, and is the universal nature of the mind."[154] As such, it "must be viewed as that generic and invariable form of knowledge of which other modes of apprehension are species."[155] According to Murti, therefore, *prajna* is "supra-rational," and on that account must also be distinguished from "the Bergsonian view of Intuition," which sees intuition as being *"instinctual"* and *"infra-rational"* in nature.[156] "It would not be very wrong," Murti argues, "to say that Bergson wants us to sink down to the level of birds and insects." But *prajna*, he concludes, "is not instinct and cannot be identified with any biotic force."[157]

Suzuki points out that *prajna* also differs radically from other intellectual forms of intuition, such as are operative, for example, in philosophical or religious discourse,[158] or in the solution of mathematical problems.[159] The difference, he says, derives in part from the fact that while the latter forms of intuition are "necessarily partial and incomplete and [do] not touch the very foundations of life considered one indivisible whole," the former (*sartori/prajna*) "must be concerned with the entirety of life," and results in a "cataclysmic," "noetic," revolution of "one's moral and spiritual life," or, in other words, "the opening of the mind-flower."[160]

The major difference between *prajna* and other intellectual forms of intuition, however, is to be found in the elimination of "logical dualism" effected by *prajna*.[161] Even though philosophical and religious intuition may be less conceptual, and more direct and immediate, than *vijnana*, it still involves, according to Suzuki, "an object of intuition known as God or reality or truth or the absolute, and the act of intuition is considered complete when a state of identification takes place between the object and the subject."[162] "But in the case of *prajna*-intuition," Suzuki concludes, "there is no definable object to be intuited."[163] A variety of objects, as insignificant as a blade of grass or a staff, may be used by a Buddhist master to demonstrate *prajna* intuition,[164] and an almost infinite variety of answers, even of a contradictory sort, might be used in response to a *koan* or *mondo*,[165] but "in *prajna*-intuition the object of intuition is never a concept postulated by an elaborate process of reasoning; it is never 'this' or 'that'."[166] In *prajna*-intuition, in other words, there is always a "key point" which "cannot be expressed as a concept, as something distinct to be placed before the mind."[167] While "*Vijnana* wants everything to be clear-cut and well defined," in *prajna*, "all is veiled in obscurity . . . something seems to be hinted at, but it is impossible to put one's finger on it."[168] That is why, as Murti notes, the sutras "speak of the intuition as unfathomable . . . immeasurable . . . and Infinite . . . inexpressible, too deep for words, too universal for distinctions to apply."[169]

In the final analysis, "the essence of *prajna*-intuition" is summed up, Suzuki observes, in the words "I do not know," given by a Buddhist monk when asked "Do you understand the Buddha-dharma (the truth or ultimate reality)?"[170] The point the monk was trying to make, Suzuki adds, was that "*prajna*-intuition really consists" in "understand[ing] what is not understandable," and "know[ing] what is unknowable."[171] What this especially implies is the impossibility of viewing one's Buddha-nature as an "object" over against oneself as the knowing "subject." "Where 'you' (the 'not-I') and 'I' are to be set apart as standing against each other," Suzuki notes, "there cannot be any *prajna*-intuition."[172] For in *prajna*, all distinctions between external and internal, or objective and subjective, are sublated, and the Buddha-reality is experienced as including both the I-Myself and Not-I-Myself.[173] "What is seen and the one who sees are identical; the seer is the seen and the seen is the seer."[174] There is not even any consciousness of the realization of Buddhahood itself, for that too would require that the thing known be distinguished from the knowing subject.[175]

While, therefore, sensory perception and *vijnana* on their own conjure up "a world of beings and non-beings," or "a world of clear-cut definitions," *prajna*-intuition yields only an experience of "emptiness" (*sunyata*)[176] and "suchness" (*tathata*).[177] What this implies is expressed succinctly in two statements in the aforementioned *Heart Sutra* to the effect that "form is emptiness" and "emptiness also is form."[178] By the first statement is apparently meant that "all phenomenal forms—trees, pencils, shouts, moods, etc.—as they really are, are empty of all the concepts by which we grasp them and fit them into our world, empty of all we project upon them."[179] The world of appearances, in other words, is altogether illusory, empty of meaning. And the "awakened one" is precisely that individual who has "gone beyond" the "world of meanings."[180] There is a danger, however, that one reduces "emptiness" itself to a "crude concept."[181] It is to head off this danger that the second statement of the sutra declares that "emptiness also is form," implying that to be genuine, the experience of *sunyata* must itself be "empty" of any concept of emptiness.[182] This is simply another way of saying that in the final analysis, *prajna* is an experience of mystery,[183] "a knowing of what is unknowable."[184]

NOTES

[1] See Angeles, *Dictionary*, 89.

[2] See *Supra*, Chapter Four; also: William P. Alston, *Perceiving God* (Ithaca and London: Cornell University Press, 1991), 34, 16,n5.

[3] See Swinburne, *The Existence of God*, 246; Michael Peterson, William Hasker, Bruce Reichenbach, and David Basinger, *Reason and Religious Belief* (New York and Oxford: Oxford University Press, 1998), 19.

[4] Alston, *Perceiving God*, 34.

[5] Swinburne, *Existence*, 246; Peterson *et. al.*, *Reason*, 2–21.

[6] Alston, *Perceiving God*, 21–22.

[7] *Ibid.*, 22.

[8] *Ibid.*

[9] See *Supra*, Chapter Three.

[10] Alston, *Perceiving God*, 26.

[11] *Ibid.*, 25.

[12] Baillie, *Sense*, 88.

[13] *Ibid.*, 260.

[14] Alston, *Perceiving God*, 61,n51.

[15] Baillie, *Sense*, 260.

[16] *Ibid.*

[17] *Ibid.*

[18] *Ibid.*, 259.

[19] *Ibid.*, 260.

[20] *Ibid.*, 259–260.

[21] *Ibid.*, 52.

[22] *Ibid.*

[23] *Ibid.*, 52–53.

[24] *Ibid.*, 53.

[25] *Ibid.*, 52–53. For Cardinal Newman's own discussion of this matter, see Newman, *Grammar of Assent*, 271.

[26] Baillie, *Sense*, 53.

[27] *Ibid.*, 54.

[28] *Ibid.*, 54. P. H. Nowell-Smith, *Ethics* (London: Penguin Books), 34.

[29] Baillie, *Sense*, 53.

[30] *Ibid.*, 64, 66.

[31] *Ibid.*, 126, 66, 67, 71.

[32] *Ibid.*, 260, 39.

[33] *Ibid.*, 88–89.

[34] *Ibid.*, 261.

[35] *Ibid.*, 1.

[36] Hick, *Faith and Knowledge*, 136,n8.

[37] *Ibid.*, 136.

[38] *Ibid.*, 137.

[39] *Ibid.*, 135.

[40] *Ibid.*

[41] *Ibid.*, 118–119.

[42] *Ibid.*, 95.

[43] *Ibid.*

[44] *Ibid.*, 115.

[45] *Ibid.*, 95–96.

[46] *Ibid.*, 96–97.

[47] *Ibid.*, 97; see also John Hick, *An Interpretation of Religion* (New Haven: Yale University Press, 1989), 140.

[48] Hick, *Faith*, 141–142; Hick, *Interpretation*, 140, 153–171.

[49] Hick, *Faith*, 142; Hick, *Interpretation*, 155.

[50] Hick, *Interpretation*, 156, 157.

[51] *Ibid.*, 165–66; also: *Ibid.*, 51, 153–154.

[52] *Ibid.*, 165.

[53] *Ibid.*, 153.

[54] *Ibid.*

[55] See Bernard J. Verkamp, "Hick's Interpretation of Religious Pluralism," *International Journal for the Philosophy of Religion* 30(1991): 103–124.

[56] Alston, *Perceiving God*, 27.

[57] *Ibid.*, 28.

[58] *Ibid.*, 27.

[59] *Ibid.*, 21.

[60] *Ibid.*, 28.

[61] *Ibid.*, 22.

[62] See *Ibid.*, 17–19; Timothy Beardsworth, *A Sense of Presence* (Oxford: The Religious Experience Research Unit, 1977).

[63] Alston, *Perceiving God*, 23.

[64] *Ibid.*

[65] *Ibid.*, 22, 23.

[66] *Ibid.*, 5, 67.

[67] *Ibid.*, 1.

[68] See Angeles, *Dictionary*, 75, 206.

[69] Alston, *Perceiving God*, 60.

[70] *Ibid.*, 20.

[71] *Ibid.*, 61,n51.

[72] *Ibid.*, 19.

[73] *Ibid.*

[74] *Ibid.*, 19–20.

[75] *Ibid.*, 20.

[76] *Ibid.*, 61.

[77] *Ibid.*, 16, 17.

[78] *Ibid.*, 52.

[79] *Ibid.*, 37.

[80] *Ibid.*, 36–37, 20.

[81] *Ibid.*, 14–15.

[82] *Ibid.*, 44.

[83] *Ibid.*

[84]   *Ibid.*, 16.

[85]   *Ibid.*, 17.

[86]   *Ibid.*

[87]   *Ibid.*, 49.

[88]   *Ibid.*

[89]   *Ibid.*, 54.

[90]   *Ibid.*, 51–53.

[91]   *Ibid.*, 16. For the context of Proudfoot's own views, see Proudfoot, *Religious Experience*, xv–xvii, 136–139.

[92]   Alston, *Perceiving God*, 14.

[93]   *Ibid.*, 37.

[94]   *Ibid.*, 37, 38.

[95]   *Ibid.*, 39.

[96]   *Ibid.*, 40–42.

[97]   *Ibid.*, 14.

[98]   *Ibid.*, 21.

[99]   *Ibid.*, 2, 29–31.

[100]   *Ibid.*, 29.

[101]   *Ibid.*, 31–32.

[102]   *Ibid.*, 32.

[103]   *Ibid.*, 21–22.

[104]   *Ibid.*, 23.

[105]   *Ibid.*, 24.

[106]   *Ibid.*; see also David Loy, *Nonduality: A Study in Comparative Philosophy* (New Haven and London: Yale University Press, 1988), 162–163.

[107]   Loy, *Nonduality*, 162; H. Brinton, *The Mystic Will* (New York: Macmillan, 1930), 100–102.

[108]   Loy, *Nonduality*, 162. Boehme's comments in this regard undoubtedly derived in part from the Aristotelian/Plotinian/Thomistic distinction between *ratio/logismos* (mere understanding, which "sees the Forms separately from each other"), and *intellectus/nous* (the faculty of intuition by which the eternal Forms are all seen together) (*Ibid.*, 162–163), which other theistic mystics such as Meister Eckhart (+1328) and Nicholas Cusa (+1464) had earlier used also to stake out a nondual kind of "pure knowing" in which "the knower *is* that which is known" (*Ibid.*, 163). Loy, it may be noted in passing, seems to have missed the fact that, as we have noted earlier, Immanuel Kant would later reverse Boehme's German terminology by associating *Verstand* with *ratio,* and attributing to it the power to categorize the data of experience, while associating *Vernunft* with *intellectus*, and ascribing to it knowledge of the transcendental ideas of God, immortality, etc. (see Copleston, *Kant*, 26, 72, 95, 142; *NCE* 14:391; *Supra*, Chapter Three).

[109]   See Loy, *Nonduality*, 295.

[110]   *Ibid.*, 294. Loy notes that "many modern theists (e.g., R. C. Zaehner, Jacques Maritain, Etienne Gilson, Joseph Marechal) have argued that the nondual experience of undifferentiated union is distinct from and inferior to the dualistic awareness of a loving God" (*Ibid.*).

[111]   Alston, *Perceiving God*, 24.

[112]   Loy, *Nonduality*, 136.

[113] Samuel Bercholz and Sherab Chodzin Kohn, eds. *Entering the Stream: An Introduction to the Buddha and His Teachings* (Boston: Shambhala, 1993), 175.

[114] *Ibid.*, 321.

[115] A "sutra" is a "thread" of "discourse of the Buddha" (*Ibid.*, 325).

[116] *Ibid.*, 154.

[117] *Ibid.*, 315.

[118] D. T. Suzuki, *Zen Buddhism: Selected Writings*, ed. By William Barrett (New York: Doubleday, 1996), 83.

[119] Bercholz, *Stream*, 315.

[120] Suzuki, *Zen*, 9, 21, 83–85.

[121] Daisetz Teitaro Suzuki, "Reason and Intuition in Buddhist Philosophy," in *Essays in East-West Philosophy*, ed. Charles A. Moore (Honolulu: University of Hawaii Press, 1951), 17–48. On the same subject, see Herbert V. Guenther, "Levels of Understanding in Buddhism," *Journal of American Oriental Society*, Volume 78.1 (January–March, 1958): 19–28; Frederick J. Streng, *Emptiness* (Nashville and New York: Abingdon Press, 1967), 82–98.

[122] Suzuki, "Reason and Intuition," 17.

[123] *Ibid.*, 23.

[124] *Ibid.*, 18.

[125] *Ibid.*, 17.

[126] *Ibid.*, 41.

[127] *Ibid.*, 18, 27.

[128] *Ibid.*, 27.

[129] *Ibid.*, 18.

[130] *Ibid.*, 17.

[131] *Ibid.*, 27.

[132] *Ibid.*, 23, 17.

[133] *Ibid.*, 23.

[134] *Ibid.*, 18.

[135] See Bercholz, *Stream,* 323.

[136] Suzuki, "Reason and Intuition," 34–35.

[137] *Ibid.*, 17.

[138] *Ibid.*, 17, 18.

[139] *Ibid.*, 41.

[140] *Ibid.*, 18.

[141] *Ibid.*, 18–20.

[142] Suzuki, *Zen*, 84.

[143] Suzuki, "Reason and Intuition," 20, 22.

[144] *Ibid.*, 22.

[145] R. R. V. Murti, *The Central Philosophy of Buddhism: A Study of the Madhyamika System* (London: George Allen and Unwin Ltd., 1968), 218.

[146] Suzuki, "Reason and Intuition," 41.

[147] *Ibid.*, 41, 22.

[148] *Ibid.*, 41; see also: Loy, *Nonduality*, 50–60.

[149] Suzuki, "Reason and Intuition," 22.

[150] Murti, *Buddhism*, 218–219.

[151] *Ibid.*, 218.
[152] Suzuki, *Zen*, 7.
[153] Suzuki, "Reason and Intuition," 24; Loy, *Nonduality*, 136.
[154] Murti, *Buddhism*, 213.
[155] *Ibid.*, 219.
[156] *Ibid.*
[157] *Ibid.*
[158] Suzuki, "Reason and Intuition," 20.
[159] Suzuki, *Zen*, 84.
[160] *Ibid.*, 84–85.
[161] *Ibid.*, 85.
[162] Suzuki, "Reason and Intuition," 20.
[163] *Ibid.*
[164] *Ibid.*, 20–21.
[165] *Ibid.*, 21; David S. Noss and John B. Noss, *A History of the World's Religions* (New York and London: Macmillan, 1990), 212.
[166] Suzuki, "Reason and Intuition," 20.
[167] *Ibid.*, 21.
[168] *Ibid.*
[169] Murti, *Buddhism*, 219.
[170] Suzuki, "Reason and Intuition," 39.
[171] *Ibid.*, 40.
[172] *Ibid.*, 21; see Noss, *Religions*, 212.
[173] See Noss, *Religions*, 212.
[174] Suzuki, "Reason and Intuition," 17, 42.
[175] Murti, *Buddhism*, 220.
[176] Suzuki, :Reason and Intuition," 34, 40; Noss, *Religions*, 202.
[177] Bercholz, *Stream*, 315.
[178] *Ibid.*, 155.
[179] *Ibid.*, 153.
[180] *Ibid.*, 154.
[181] *Ibid.*
[182] *Ibid.*
[183] Suzuki, "Reason and Intuition," 21, 46.
[184] *Ibid.*, 40.

CHAPTER SIX

Conclusion

Having explained in an earlier work what constitutes the "object" of the religious sense, I have been primarily concerned in this study with investigating its more formal, subjective side, and seeing how a religious sense might be interpreted. Not every conceivable interpretation in this regard has been reviewed. But among the many possibilities, the following have been identified as the most significant to have been propounded by past and present thinkers.

In the first place, it has been seen that according to some interpreters of religion, the religious sense can best be defined as an evolutionarily produced biological instinct or genetic propensity. While under the influence of environmental factors in its stimulation and development, and while subject to interaction with other instincts and the play of reason, the religious sense, so conceived, is said to be innate, and ontogenetically speaking, prior to any kind of sense experience. Either through the genetic transmission of accidental congenital variations as fixed features of the species, or through the inheritance of habits cultivated in the process of the species adapting to its environment, all humans are supposedly born with brains programed to process the raw data of sense experience in accordance with certain epigenetic rules in such a way as to perceive the mysterious dimensions of reality and to experience on that account a certain pleasurable feeling of wonder that, without any previous education, foresight, or choice, simultaneously inclines an individual to both flee and draw near the mysterious object encountered. Whatever knowledge is involved in such an instinctive feeling of wonder, it is always "dim and vague," "preconceptual," and "inarticulate." The mystery of reality is "recognized" or "perceived," but not comprehended or conceptualized.

87

The second group of thinkers would also have us interpret the religious sense as an instinct—but as one that is spiritual rather than biological. From the perspective of a dualistic interpretation of the relation of the human body and soul as two separate and independent substances, the religious sense is defined as a "natural light" whereby any human mind, as a faculty of the soul that may itself have been subject to evolutionary influences, is structured or predisposed either to discover within itself, upon coming of age, and barring any sickness, abnormality or self-imposed obstacle, certain ideas of God and the mystery of reality such as have been implicit from birth, or at least to fashion such ideas out of reflection upon itself prior to, albeit not necessarily independent of, sense experience. Although such virtually innate ideas anticipate conceptual knowledge, they differ radically from the latter, it is said, to the extent of being instinctive, spontaneous, direct, immediate, universal, necessary, and indisputable. "Clear and distinct," as they might be, they cannot "comprehend" the ultimate mystery of reality. "God" is perceived, but not comprehended, remaining always an object of wonder, an "idea of mystery."

Eschewing any dualistic separation of body and soul, and assuming along Kantian lines instead an understanding of mind as the subjective principle by which the self organizes the data of experience, the third group of thinkers interpret the religious sense as a categorical disposition of every human mind, through a process similar to Platonic *anamnesis* and Kant's aesthetic judgment, to subsume the form of one or another particular object under the "essential idea," the "secret divine plan," the ultimate "mystery" of reality. When such a faculty of divination is actualized—and it is admitted that not all or even most human beings choose to do so—there arises, it is said, a "numinous feeling," a "feeling of the supernatural," a feeling for the "mysterious presence of the Infinite in the Finite, the Eternal in the Temporal." This feeling is cognitive, but only in the intuitive manner of poetic imagination or pious contemplation. It delivers a pleasurable glimpse of the conformity of the object's form with the "essential idea" underlying the "sheer overplus" of Nature's "totality," but there is no analytical or logical conception, no discursive thought, involved. The knowledge it brings is direct, immediate, and original, like the "simple vision" of a child. Precisely because it envisions the ultimate mystery of "eternal reality breaking through the veil of temporal existence," its "cognition" will always remain "dim and inexpressible."

While agreeing with Kant on the active role of an animated brain, a fourth group of thinkers tries to escape the skepticism about noumenal reality resulting supposedly from Kant's exclusive focus on the conceptualist organization of the data of sensible intuition by picking up on Fichte's comment about the human intellect's "spiritual dynamism," and interpreting the religious sense in terms of what Thomas Aquinas had said about "the drive of the active intellect to the Infinite God." As the locus of a single process of two inseparable moments of abstraction and conversion to the phantasm, the cogitative power of the human intellect, it is said, spontaneously "actualizes" the "potential intelligibility" of the particular sense image by subsuming it under the universal law of "being" that is intuited in the "light" of the knowing subject's "original awareness" or "self-presence." Such awareness is said to generate a "preapprehension" or "anticipation" of Being precisely to the extent that it involves the knowing subject in a discovery in itself of an insatiable desire to know, or of itself as "a question to which there is no answer."

Because every answer is always just the beginning of a new question, the knowing subject finds itself open to "everything," which is not the "nothingness" of the absurdist vision of reality, but "the whole in its unity and totality"—what western philosophy has traditionally designated as "being," and what most religions have called the "holy mystery" or "God." The knowledge of God resulting from such an intuitive grasp of the knowing subject's "radical openness" or "spirituality" is said to be "transcendental" and "original" in the sense of being the "permanent existential" and *a priori* "ground" of every human act of knowing. But in itself it carries no positive, concrete, or determinate content. There is no direct and immediate insight into the nature of God. Nor does it involve any inference of God's existence from observation of the cosmos. God is known "only in the mode of otherness and distance." Any such knowledge, therefore, is also "prereflective," "unthematic," "preconceptual," and "anonymous" to the extent that its "term" can never become one object among other objects, and will forever remain "incomprehensible," "ineffable," "indefinable," and "nameless," notwithstanding any subsequent elaboration along mythological, metaphysical, and analogical lines. And finally, such knowledge is also said to be "passive and receptive" in the sense that its term is not the product of man's own ideation, but "the infinite horizon of being making itself manifest."

The fifth and final group of thinkers were those who interpret the religious sense in experiential terms as an awareness of an encounter with God. Such awareness, it is said, will vary in accordance with the level or grade of immediacy with which the object of the religious experience presents itself. In those cases where God is "presented" in (not deduced, or inferred from) some other object of perception, like the beauty of nature, the biblical word, a sermon, the voice of conscience, an everyday encounter, or an event of human history, the religious sense is said to consist of an innate faculty or "inner sense," which, when actualized, gives rise to "faith" or a "primary mode of awareness," wherein ambiguous natural, historical, and social events are "experienced as" being "mysterious" or "other and greater than [they] seem," or, in other words, as a "presence of the divine." To what extent such a "mediate perception" involves conceptualized interpretation is a matter of debate. But those championing it insist that whatever interpretation might be involved, the "immediacy" of the divine presence is not compromised. It is "God" himself whom one encounters, not just some "sign" of God. And the "awareness," therefore, is intuitive and direct, not the product of either deductive or inductive discursive thinking.

In other cases where the immediacy of the divine presence is "mediated" through a state of consciousness, or, in other words, where God is "presented" to human consciousness in the same immediate way in which objects in the environment are presented to one's consciousness in sense perception, the religious sense is said to consist of a "spiritual" sensitivity, which, when activated, affords the religious person a "putative," generally "non-sensory," "direct awareness" or "mystical perception" of the divine presence. Like sense perception, to which it is thought to be analogous, such an awareness is said to differ radically from "thinking," "calling up mental images," "entertaining propositions," or "reasoning" about God. In sharp contrast to abstract thinking, but again like sense perception, it is said to be a mode of consciousness in which the object of the experience (God/Mystery) is present with distinctive, albeit indefinable, "nonaffective phenomenal *qualia*." Although susceptible to being colored by the religious person's own conceptual scheme, it is also said to be, in and of itself, essentially independent of conceptualization, and as such something more than a merely subjective experience overlaid with rational explanation. In still other cases of so-called "extreme mystical experience," where the "immediacy" of the divine presence is thought to be "absolute," or, in other words, without the mediation of even a state of consciousness, the religious sense is interpreted as a "higher [i.e., non-specialized] faculty" which, when "awakened," inclines the human mind to abandon any discursive, bifurcating process of abstract thinking, and to surrender instead to the more spontaneous, intuitive way of knowing that leaves no room for reflection, analysis, interpretation, deliberation, or logical progression from premises to conclusions. In the sweep of such "transcendental wisdom," human consciousness is said to be carried completely beyond all distinctions of subject and object, and absorbed in the undifferentiated unity of the "Godhead," or, as some would prefer to put it, in the ultimate "emptiness." It is the wisdom of "knowing what is unknowable."

The radical differences between these interpretations render nearly impossible any attempt to bring them all into some harmonious unity. But for all their variety, there is also much that these different interpretations have in common. In the first place, it may be noted that most of them interpret the religious sense as some kind of higher faculty by which humans can discover something more in reality than can be ascribed to nature itself. In doing so, they were not talking merely about the general capacity of the human mind to collect, process, or store data and information of any and every sort. If that were all they were trying to say, their conclusions in this regard would have been trivial and of little epistemological or any other interest. But, in fact, they had in mind to say much more. Whether they described the religious faculty as a natural instinct, an epigenetic rule, a genetic program, a spiritual instinct or natural light, a virtually innate idea, an archetypal aptitude, a category of the mind, a structure of consciousness, an intentionality, an inner sense, a third eye, or a Buddha-nature, they were all suggesting that just as the consciousness of an animal might be structured in such a way as to make it especially sensitive to sounds of a particular sort that escape human detection, so human consciousness enjoys a unique potency, tendency, disposition, or propensity toward the active reception of the mysterious overtones of reality.

In saying that humans enjoy such a faculty, these thinkers did not mean to imply that every human being actually makes use of it. They recognized that immaturity, laziness, distraction, preoccupation, prejudice, and many other personal, cultural, and environmental factors might hinder its actualization altogether, or at least influence the level of its development in any one or another individual. They were also convinced, however, that even if the growth of the religious sense has been stunted in some individuals, or allowed to atrophy in others, those same individuals nonetheless still retain a basic disposition toward experiencing the mystery of reality. For such a faculty, they thought, is something more than a mere habit resulting from the individual's interaction with his or her environment. In their view, the religious sense is rather something that humans are born with, something innate, and not merely a cultural product that the individual acquires through experience. Repeatedly, they say that the human mind is not at birth a mere *tabula rasa* or blank tablet that is totally passive to the experiential data it encounters. Anticipating or confirming the Kantian emphasis upon the active role of the human mind in constituting the object of human knowledge, they all insist that while the mind may need to be triggered to experience, and convert all its insights into imaginary terms, it can and does nonetheless shape the data of experience in accordance with certain of its own "given" or "*a priori*" structures, one of which is the religious sense of mystery. Humans are not, therefore, in the view of the thinkers under consideration, "neutral" by birth as far as religion goes. While readily acknowledging that the religious sense can, like the aesthetic or any other sense, be neglected or even killed by the exercise of individual choice, they nonetheless insist that all humans come into this world already inclined to envision reality against the religious horizon of mystery.

To say that individual human beings are born with a religious sense does not, of course, preclude the possibility that, phylogenetically speaking, the human species has learned from experience to interpret reality in terms of mystery. And some of the thinkers reviewed above no doubt prefer to think that something of that sort is exactly what happened in the past, namely, that in the process of adapting to their environment, our ancestors enhanced their chances of survival by way of cultivating a habit of envisioning "something more" in the world of their experience (e.g., by differentiating sacred and profane dimensions of reality), and through natural selection eventually came to pass such a habit on to their progeny in the form of an ontogenetically innate faculty. But most of the other thinkers reviewed have been seen to have argued that human beings have been religious from the very start, and that if, as some readily admit, the religious sense of mystery has an instinctive base as a result of man's animal past, any such instinct underwent radical alteration from the very beginning of mankind as a result of its having been brought under the influence of the human soul.

Common to most of the thinkers reviewed is also the recognition that when actualized the religious sense consists of a certain knowledge of the mysterious reality experienced. More often than not, such knowledge is called a "preapprehension," a "primary apprehension," or "original knowledge," in the sense of being the "source," the beginning and end, of all human knowledge.[1] Such knowledge is also said by most of the thinkers reviewed to be "unthematic" and "preconceptual." Not all go to the extent of trying to put a stop to "thinking" altogether (as do many of the Buddhists), or even so far as putting "reason" down (as did not a few of the Romantic poets). Nor will most of them conclude, therefore, that the kind of knowledge delivered by an actualized religious sense must consist of a totally non-dualistic "consciousness without an object," such as is championed by certain traditions of extreme mysticism. But even those thinkers who recognize the need for "reflection," and allow some room for theological or philosophical thought and talk about the ultimate mystery of reality, readily admit that the "primary apprehension" we have of the latter is "unthematic" and "preconceptual." It is "unthematic," in the sense that it carries no determinate content, and tells us nothing positive about that which is known. At best it is but an "inkling," a "presage," and "anticipation" of the mystery that is being experienced by the religious person. The knowledge is "pre-conceptual" to the extent of being prior to, and ultimately beyond, any attempt to have it explained in objective terms.

Most of the thinkers reviewed also insist that such "primary apprehension" is "intuitive." The knowledge it delivers is not something one infers by way of discursive thinking of either an inductive or deductive sort. To be sure, whether one thinks of it in instinctive, innatist, or whatever terms, such knowledge may need to be triggered by stimuli other than the ultimate mystery itself (i.e., "God"). But even in a case where the awareness of mystery is "mediated" by an awareness of some other "object," the knowledge involved is said to come directly and immediately.

Although "dim and obscure," because of its "preconceptual" and "intuitive" nature, the knowledge resulting from the actualization of the religious sense is also said to enjoy a high degree of certitude. The conviction it carries, however, is not necessarily of the sort associated with verification by empirical observation. Nor does it always rely on immunity from falsification by scientific experimentation. Correspondence of its content with the "facts" is not the sole, or even the primary, test of its "truth." Its pragmatic value—how it contributes to the survival of one or another population, how it "works" to help humans realize their potential, how it inspires human creativity, an appreciation for beauty, a concern for justice, a passion for peace, etc. —or the way it coheres with what else we know and brings all the disparate pieces of the latter into a big and unified picture, may count more toward the appraisal of its truth than the extent to which it "mirrors" the material surface of reality. The personal, "experiential" (as opposed to "empirical") nature of such knowledge is also thought to contribute to its reliability. More often than not, the thinkers under consideration will claim to know "in their heart" that to which they are attesting with such conviction, namely the mysterious dimensions of reality. An actual "encounter" of the latter in either personal or impersonal terms has left them with the "feeling" for the truth, even though it may be beyond their ability or interest to try proving the same to anyone else.

Finally, then, it may be noted that most of the thinkers reviewed in previous chapters generally describe the knowledge resulting from the actualization of the religious sense as being of an emotional sort. None seem to have any problem with admitting the possibility of an emotion being cognitive. What exactly such a religiously cognitive emotion consists of, however, is another question, to which a variety of answers are given. But common to almost all of the thinkers reviewed is the assumption that in the final analysis, the cognitive emotion involved in the religious sense consists, if not exclusively, at least to a very significant degree, in the feeling of wonder. But what exactly is to be understood thereby, and what it implies about the nature of the religious sense, was not always spelled out in the immediate context of their discussion. It might be helpful, therefore, to try to do so in the concluding pages of this study.

Traditionally, the feeling of wonder has generally been thought to preclude any dogmatic claim to omniscience. The "gods," Plato argued, are incapable of wondering to the extent that they already know everything.[2] Human beings, like the young mathematician Theaetetus in the Socratic dialogue of the same name, on the other hand, are said to be able to wonder precisely because there is much in reality about which they are "perplexed."[3] The whole goal of the Socratic dialectic and its use of irony, therefore, was to arouse a sense of wonder and a love of wisdom (i.e., "philein-sophia") by shocking individuals into an awareness of their own ignorance.[4] Aristotle's use of methodical doubt (aporia) to shock "fools" out of their "self-satisfaction" rested on the same assumption—the assumption, namely, that wonder arises out of the experience of human ignorance.[5] Human beings "originally began to wonder," Aristotle wrote, "at the obvious difficulties about the greater matters, e.g., about the phenomena of the moon and those of the sun and of the stars, and about the genesis of the universe. And a man who is puzzled and wonders thinks himself ignorant."[6] In Aristotle's view, we have knowledge of something only to the extent that we know its "cause."[7] "One wonders," then, Thomas Aquinas would later write in his commentary on Aristotle's *Metaphysics*, "when one sees effects whose cause is hidden from him,"[8] or, as Thomas added in other passages, "when . . . the cause . . . surpasses his knowledge or power of understanding," or is "other than he had thought it to be."[9] Summarizing this whole line of thought, Descartes would later comment that the object of wonder is that which "we have previously been ignorant of,"[10] or, in other words, that which is "rare," "extraordinary," and "new, or very different from what we knew in the past or from what we supposed it was going to be."[11]

To say, therefore, that the religious sense, when actualized, consists of a feeling of wonder is to imply, first of all, that individuals are radically ignorant of the "object" of their religious experience. It reinforces whatever else has been said about the "mysterious" (i.e., "ineffable," "incomprehensible," "indefinable") nature of such an object, or about the "unthematic" and "preconceptual" character of whatever knowledge there is accompanying the "original" moment of religious experience.

The "ignorance" traditionally associated with wonder is not to be confused, however, with "nescience." By "nescience" is understood the complete negation of knowledge, such as would preclude any possibility of its removal, as well as any awareness of its existence.[12] Brute animals, for example, are not only inherently and irremediably incapable of ever knowing the causes of things, they are also lacking in any awareness of their lack of knowledge. To that extent, they are said to be incapable also of ever experiencing wonder[13] (contrary to the claims of the Cambridge Platonist, Henry More, that "at the sight of the sun or moon," apes and elephants display a "strange sense of . . . Wonderment, near to that Passion which in us is called Veneration").[14] For, as Josef Pieper has noted, and as Socrates so clearly demonstrated, "to wonder is not merely not to know; it means to be inwardly aware and sure that one does not know, and that one understands oneself in not knowing."[15] Furthermore, the lack of knowledge involved in wonder is only partial.[16] As Descartes especially emphasized, something is experienced as "wonderful" only because it differs "from what we knew in the past or from what we supposed it was going to be."[17] We wonder, in other words, not because we are completely ignorant about the object of our experience, but because what we now see or hear is not altogether in line with what we have seen or heard before. For Descartes, as well as for Thomas and the other aforementioned thinkers, the ignorance associated with wonder often comes down, then, to what L. M. Regis has described as "the intellect's inability to see why two accounts are incompossible when each of them seems to be comprehensible and to contain elements of truth."[18] Finally, it should be noted, that in contrast to the incorrigible nature of nescience, the ignorance associated with wonder is said to be of a sort that can be corrected to some extent through a process of learning.[19]

Whether the likes of Aristotle, Descartes, and Hegel carried this latter assertion to the point of reducing wonder to nothing more than "puzzlement" or "mental confusion" that can be overcome through science, as Hannah Arendt and others have claimed,[20] will be seen to be at least debatable. But, like Thomas Aquinas and others, they certainly did conceive of wonder as part of "man's natural desire to know."[21] What makes wondering such a pleasure, Aristotle wrote, was the fact that it "implies the desire of learning" the "cause" of things "in order to escape ignorance."[22] And not just the cause of some particular things, but the "highest cause," the "cause of everything and of all things . . . the 'whither' and the 'whence,' the origin and the end, the plan and the structure, the framework and the meaning of reality."[23] Commenting on Aristotle, Thomas concluded similarly that "wonder arises in men," not just because of ignorance, but because "in every man there resides a natural desire to know the cause of any effect which he sees."[24] Wonder, then, according to Thomas, gives rise to "inquiry": "For instance, if a man, knowing the eclipse of the sun, consider that it must be due to some cause, and know not what that cause is, he wonders about it, and from wondering proceeds to inquire. Nor does this inquiry cease until he arrive at a knowledge of the essence of the cause."[25] Thus, wonder, Thomas continues (again citing Aristotle), "is the beginning of wisdom, being as it were, the road to the search of truth," and it is "pleasurable" precisely because "it includes the desire of learning the cause . . . the hope of getting the knowledge which one desires to have . . . [and] learn[ing] something new, that is, that the cause is other than he had thought it to be."[26]

Thomas does, it should be noted in this regard, sometimes distinguish between "wonder" (*admiratio*) and "astonishment" (*stupor*), and observes that while the former initiates a pursuit of wisdom, the latter "is a hindrance to it."[27] Descartes picks up on the same distinction between "wonder" (*L'admiration*) and "astonishment" (*L'etonnement*),[28] and warns against the danger of "astonishment" getting in the way of the pursuit of science.[29] By "astonishment" he means "an excess of wonder."[30] What can happen, he notes, is that the "surprise" we experience upon encountering something "new, rare, and extraordinary" can be so great that it makes the "entire body remain immobile like a statue, and renders one incapable either of perceiving anything of the object but the face first presented or, consequently, of acquiring a more specific knowledge of it"[31]; it "makes one fix one's attention solely on the first image of presented objects without acquiring any other knowledge of them," and "this is what prolongs the sickness of the blindly curious—that is, those who investigate rarities only to wonder at them and not to understand them"[32]; it "can entirely eradicate or pervert the use of reason."[33] But too little wonder (as in the case of the "dull and stupid who do not have a constitutional inclination toward Wonder"[34]) can also be a problem, Descartes notes.[35] While, then, we should try "to emancipate ourselves . . . as much as possible" from an excess of wonder, "it is good," he adds, "to be born with some inclination to this passion, since it disposes us to the acquisition of the sciences."[36]

That the religious sense reaches a climax in a feeling of wonder, therefore, should not be taken to mean that individuals so disposed are obscurantists who are either oblivious to, or altogether resigned to, the complete and incorrigible nature of their ignorance. Quite to the contrary, while emerging from an awareness of their lack of knowledge, their wonder is excited no less by a natural desire to deepen and broaden the "original knowledge" afforded them by their encounter with the mysterious object of their religious experience. As an embodiment of wonder, the religious sense, in other words, can thrive only where there is a genuine desire to learn. Whether such a *desiderium sciendi* can ever be satisfied, however, is another question.

As noted earlier, the comments of Aristotle, Descartes, and Hegel about the possibility of overcoming the ignorance associated with wonder have often been interpreted to mean that wonder can be reduced to mere "puzzlement" that can and will inevitably be resolved. But such interpretations are doubtful. For, while it may very well have been the case that Cartesian science had as its goal to reduce wonder at natural phenomena, Descartes did nonetheless recommend wonder "at God and at oneself, in respect of a quality that, in a way, makes us like God," or, in other words, at the realm beyond which physics can touch.[37] And in view of the emphasis put by both Aristotle and Hegel on the "unattainable wisdom" pursued in the "divine science" of metaphysics,[38] it is doubtful if either had in mind to altogether strip reality of its mysterious veil, or to reduce the object of wonder to nothing more than a "problem" awaiting solution.[39] But however one might interpret the thinking of these three philosophers, it certainly was not the intention of Thomas Aquinas to suggest that the ignorance of wonder will ever be totally overcome. As many of his interpreters have pointed out, Thomas was keenly aware of the ultimate mystery of reality, and especially of the Godhead. Even in the end, in the so-called beatific vision, our knowledge will remain, it is said, a vision of "divine darkness," an "understanding of non-understanding."[40] What this implies, of course, is that the more we come to know the object of wonder, the more wonderful or mysterious it becomes, with the result that notwithstanding our knowledge, it always remains beyond our comprehension. Whatever glimpse of "being" or the "wholeness of reality" a sense of wonder might afford one, it always remains, as Jerome Miller has noted from a Lonergarian/Heideggerian perspective, "a knowledge of Being *as Unknown*."[41]

The wonder to which an experience of Being gives rise, therefore, is not, Miller goes on to explain, so much an act of exploiting revelations, dreams, or intuitions, to leap beyond the limits of our current understanding,[42] as it is rather an act of loving surrender to the mystery of reality, a hopeful plunge into the very abyss of our radical ignorance.[43] In the final analysis, it means finding the trust, as did Abraham ("the father of faith," according to Christian writers) "to go out not knowing where he was going" (Hebrews, 11:8).

Consistent with Jesus' well-known admonition that only childlike faith can gain one admission to the kingdom of God (Luke, 18:17), Miller, like Lonergan,[44] compares the act of wonder to the venturesome spirit of inquiry that typifies the reaction of children to their new found world. Picking up on Jacques Derrida's imagery of "hinge and door,"[45] Miller proceeds to describe the "phenomenological structure of wonder" by analyzing "wondrous" childhood experiences as "venturing into a secret room, or exploring an uninhabited house, or even opening the lid of a chest hidden in the attic and found unexpectedly."[46] What is most remarkable about such experiences, he says, is that in the "intimations of being" they provided, there was never any "illusion of understanding what being means."[47] What really "fascinates and terrifies" the child "is the unknown in its very character as unknown," or, in other words, the impossibility of homologizing "what lies behind the door with the contents of her small but familiar universe."[48] "Wonder," then, "is already the rupture of the same by the other, where the other is simply the unknown itself in its difference from the known."[49] But even after opening the door and gaining "access to what is on the other side of it," the child, like the "explorer," remains "caught in the throe of wonder," because "wonder is the hinge that opens up the absolute future," with the result that "for her the familiar is constantly turning into the strange, the obvious into the questionable, the it of immediacy into the it to be known only through inquiry."[50]

The child will continue to marvel "over the very things that [are] closest to hand and most familiar,"[51] precisely because its "wonder does not refer [her] to that object in its givenness," but rather "surprises her into realizing that, as perfectly as the object is given to [her], [she] [does] not know what it is."[52] Far from "mirroring" what "is present in the present,"[53] the child's wonder "effaces the image of the given,"[54] opens the eyes of the child to a dream-like, imaginary world of the future,[55] and, precisely through the "playfulness of the moment," draws her on into the "wholly other" realm of "Being."[56] "Being is not the from-which of the child's wonder; it is the toward-which."[57] The child's "intimations of being," therefore, are also and simultaneously "intimations of the sacred: that which, beyond us, other than us, it would be utterly dreadful to know; a mystery that beckons even as it horrifies, an other which bids us approach at the very moment we find it to be most forbidding."[58] Contrary to what might have been implied by Auguste Comte's hostile utterances about the "infantile" character of religion,[59] the child's wondrous "intimations of the sacred" actually incline the child to "leave its childhood behind" and "to risk opening even that door whose hinge makes a terrifying sound, as if to warn her . . . of death itself."[60] If, therefore, as Kierkegaard claimed, wonder gives way to "worship,"[61] it is the worship of a man already come of age.

As Pieper notes, however, there is a danger that as humans grow up and go to work, they succumb to what he, like Rahner, calls the "bourgeois mentality."[62] In the *Symposium*, Plato ascribed such a mentality to the businessmen who accost the young and supposedly "crazed" Apollodorus, and try to pry out of him what Socrates and others had said about love during the banquet that had been held recently in the poet Agathon's house.[63] It is clear from Plato's account that these businessmen were very impressed with their ability "to get things done" by way of manufacturing and selling products. They apparently cared very little about the truth or philosophical meaning of the speeches, and were only interested in finding out who had made the wittiest and most elegant of speeches, and won the argument. Plato has Apollodorus heap scorn upon their bourgeois attitude.[64]

Not only businessmen, but anyone—philosophers and theologians included—succumb to the bourgeois mentality, according to Pieper, when they "accept [their] environment defined as it is by the immediate needs of life, so completely and finally that things happening cannot any longer become transparent."[65] Ordinary things of everyday life become opaque and are viewed in their disconnected isolation as being nothing more than commodities to be bought and sold, pleasurable objects of immediate gratification, or items of consumption.[66] That individuals addicted to this bourgeois mentality are now and then surprised by one or another sensational event, is only another indication, Pieper observes, of the "deadened sense of wonder."[67] They have lost their sense of wonder, because, he says, they have lost their souls.[68] The "soul," according to Aristotle and his medieval commentators, is in a certain sense "everything that is"—in the sense, namely, that it knowingly places itself in relation to the whole of being.[69] To be a spirit or soul, therefore, meant in the tradition of Western philosophy "to exist in the midst of the whole of reality," "to relate to the totality of existing things."[70] Losing one's soul, then, was equivalent, in the final analysis, to losing contact with the whole of reality. And to lose contact with the whole of reality is to veer from the path of wonder, or, in other words, to lose one's religious sense of direction.

Finally, it might be asked whether wonder is actually of an inherently religious nature, or whether it is not, perhaps, more immediately a product of philosophy. It will be recalled, for example, how Socrates, upon being confronted with Theaetetus' amazement at the apparent inconsistencies resulting from the application of various principles, exclaimed: "I see, my dear Theaetetus, that Theodorus had a true insight into your nature when he said that you were a philosopher, for wonder is the feeling of a philosopher, and philosophy begins in wonder."[71] Aristotle made a similar point in the first book of his *Metaphysics* when he wrote that "it is owing to their wonder that men both now begin and at first began to philosophize."[72] And commenting on this Aristotelian passage, Thomas Aquinas noted that the "reason why the philosopher may be likened to the poet is this: both are concerned with that which is wonderful."[73] Statements of this sort might leave one with the impression that wonder belongs more to philosophy than it does to religion. But that would be a wrong impression. For as Pieper has emphatically noted, the concern for the world *as a whole*, which has characterized perennial philosophy, and which, as we have seen in previous chapters, lies at the heart of the experience of mystery and the wonder it engenders, is not something conjured up by the first philosophers.[74] It represents rather an "interpretation of the world," or a "wisdom" that, as Plato and Aristotle put it, has been "handed down by the ancients," who, in turn, had received it from on high.[75]

Aristotle only hints at what he means thereby when he suggests that "the lover of myth is in a sense a lover of Wisdom, for the myth is composed of wonders."[76] But Plato is quite explicit. Referring, for example, to the divine origin of his doctrine of ideas, Plato wrote that this "knowledge came down to us like a flame of light, as a gift from the Gods, I am convinced, brought to us by the hand of some unknown Prometheus from a divine source—and the ancients, being better than we are, and nearer to the Gods, handed this tradition down to us."[77] The wonder-causing, mythological and uncritical, interpretation of the world in its totality, therefore, is, according to Plato, a "divine wisdom," a seeing of the whole of reality from a divine perspective, and existing "from time immemorial," "long before man began to philosophize."[78] It is a "gift," something "given" *prior* to any human effort at thought.[79] As such, wonder, according to Plato, is the "beginning of philosophy," not only in the sense of being its "starting point" (*initium*) but in the sense also of being its "*principium*, the lasting source, the *fons et origo*."[80] In addition to being the "impulse and impetus" that gets philosophy started,[81] it is also the "end" to which the dialectic must inevitably surrender.[82]

Not all historians, it should be noted, would subscribe to such an accounting of the origin of philosophy. As Pieper has observed, some historians, "under the impulse of rationalistic and 'progressive' doctrine," have located the beginning of philosophy at precisely that moment "when thought cut itself free from [religious] tradition,"[83] or, in other words, during the pre-Socratic period when Solon, Thales, Anaximander, and especially Xenophanes, supposedly had in mind to "enlighten" their contemporaries by subjecting the mythology of Homer and Hesiod to "critical reflection and innovative speculation."[84] On the basis of such an interpretation it has come to be assumed that "rebellion against religious tradition" is "at the very core of Western philosophy."[85]

But against such an interpretation of historical events, others have argued that it was precisely against the already "enlightened" (i.e., "fictionalized") character of Homeric mythology that the pre-Socratics were protesting, and that their "penetrating analysis" was an attempt, as Mircea Eliade claims, to strip the Homeric mythology of its super-ficially "fictional" form, and search out its ontological and allegorical allusions,[86] or, as Pieper puts it, "to return to a more primitive, 'traditional,' pre-Homeric theology,"[87] on the assumption that only by preserving the feeling of wonder generated by religion could philosophy itself hope to survive. Far from being true to the critical analysis of the first philosophers, therefore, it could be argued that the attempt by modern rationalistic/empiricism to put a new spin on the old Stoic aphorism "not to wonder at anything"[88] by trying to "demystify" all of reality,[89] is actually a distortion that constitutes a serious threat to the very survival of philosophy, or for that matter, of science and any other human endeavor that might conceivably feed off of the religious sense and its concomitant feeling of wonder.

NOTES

[1] It should be noted that the "primary" or "original" knowledge referred to here does not necessarily preclude, but also is not synonymous with, what Lucien Levy-Bruhl called the "primitive mentality" whereby "the primitive 'participates' in the mystic nature of all that surrounds him . . . lives in the seen and the unseen worlds simultaneously, [and shows] indifference to the law of contradiction" (Lucien Levy-Bruhl, *Primitive Mentality* [Boston: Beacon Press, 1966], 5).

[2] Plato, *Symposium*, 204: *GB* 7:164. Thomas Aquinas wrote similarly that God cannot wonder because he has "no ignorance of causes" (*In Matt. Lectura*, c.8, v.10: as cited in Guy Godin, "La notion d'admiration," *Laval Theologique et Philosophique* XVII.1[1961]:49).

[3] Plato, *Theaetetus*, 155: *GB* 7:519.

[4] Plato, *Meno*, 71: *GB* 7:174. Plato has Diotima say in the *Symposium* that the real evil of ignorance "is the fact that he who is neither good nor wise is nevertheless satisfied with himself: he has no desire for that of which he feels no want" (*Symposium*, 204: *GB* 7:164).

[5] See Aristotle, *Metaphysics*, Bk III, 1: 995a–b: *GB* 8:513. See also: *NCE* 1: 678–679; 4:1023.

[6] Aristotle, *Metaphysics* Bk I, 2, 982b, 11–20: *GB* 8: 500–501.

[7] *Ibid.*, Bk I, 1–4, 980a–984b: *GB* 8: 499–503.

[8] Thomas, *In 1 Meta.* 3.55, as cited in *NCE* 14:1004.

[9] Thomas, *ST* I–II, 32, 8: *GB* 19:764–765.

[10] Descartes, *Passions of the Soul*, Part II, Art. 75, p. 59.

[11] *Ibid.*, II, 53, p. 52; II, 70, p. 56; II, 76, p. 61; II, 78, p. 61; II, 150, p. 103; II, 197, p. 125.

[12] See L. M. Regis, *Epistemology* (New York: Macmillan, 1959), 15–16; also: Thomas, *ST* I–II, 76, 2.

[13] Josef Pieper, *Leisure, The Basis of Culture,* translated by Alexander Dru (New York and Toronto: The New American Library, 1963), 104; Regis, *Epistemology*, 15.

[14] As cited in Harrison, '*Religion*', 44–45.

[15] Pieper, *Leisure*, 101.

[16] Regis, *Epistemology*, 15.

[17] Descartes, *Passions*, II, 53, p. 52.

[18] Regis, *Epistemology*, 15, 17, 29, 35, 39. For Descartes himself, Regis notes, the object of wonder became "the fact that there are two tellers" (i.e., the one same mind telling two different stories) (*Ibid.*, 35, 40, 44). Regis uses this insight to structure his discussion of the "modern epistemological problem" as posed by Descartes, Kant, and Neo-Scholastic thinkers such as L. Noel and Joseph Maréchal (*Ibid.*, 32–108).

[19] Pieper, *Leisure*, 103.

[20] Arendt, *Life of the Mind* I, 114, 143; Pieper, *Leisure*, 102, 109.

[21] See Aristotle, *Metaphysics*, Bk I, 1, 980a: *GB* 8:499, and Pieper, *Leisure*, 103.

[22] Aristotle, *Rhetoric* Bk I, 11: 1371a, 31: *GB* 9:614; *Metaphysics* Bk I, 2: 983a, 15–20: *GB* 8:501.

[23] Pieper, *Leisure*, 110.

[24] *ST* I, 12, 1; *GB* 19:51; *ST* I–II, 3, 8: *GB* 19:629; *ST* I–II, 32, 8: *GB* 19:764.

[25] *ST* I–II, 3, 8: *GB* 19:629.

[26] *ST* I–II, 32, 8: *GB* 19: 764–765.

[27] *ST* I–II, 41, 4, ad 5: *GB* 19:801. In line with the traditional definition of the Latin term *stupor*, I am translating it as "astonishment," instead of the English stupor, so as to avoid confusing it with the use of the latter term by modern writers such as Rudolf Otto to refer to a sense of mystery. Thomas himself defined *stupor* as a "species of fear" which arises when man encounters some "unaccustomed evil" (*ST* I–II, 41, 4: *GB* 19:800–801). He seems to mean that such an individual is so "startled" that he is unable to pursue any inquiry.

[28] Descartes, *Passions* II, 53 and 54, p. 52; see also the illustration of the two different attitudes on p. 60.

[29] *Ibid.*, II, 76 and 78, pp. 59–61.

[30] *Ibid.*, II, 73 and 78, pp. 58, 61.

[31] *Ibid.*, II, 73, p. 58.

[32] *Ibid.*, II, 78, p.61.

[33] *Ibid.*, II, 76, pp. 59–60.

[34] *Ibid.*, II, 77, p. 61.

[35] *Ibid.*, II, 76, pp. 59–61.

[36] *Ibid.*, II, 76, p. 60.

[37] *Ibid.*, 61,n17.

[38] See Aristotle, *Metaphysics* Bk I, 2: 983a, 1–25: *GB* 8:501; Pieper, *Leisure*, 108, 110–111. Jerome Miller, it may be noted, argues from a post-modern perspective that the classical, Aristotelian "metaphysics of presence" remains a threat to genuine wonder even if it is admitted that "the parousia of presence is unattainable," for "one is still using it as one's absolute reference point if one understands one's position in terms of its deferral. Even when we admit that thought is moving toward an always receding destination, we continue to plot its course in exclusively horizontal terms, i.e., exclusively in terms of destinations to be reached, distances to be traversed, horizons to be thematized, absences to be presented, concealments to be revealed. To append a

warning that none of these projected closures can ever be achieved does not alter the fact that closure remains the governing objective" (Jerome Miller, *In the Throe of Wonder: Intimations of the Sacred in a Post-Modern World* [Albany, N.Y.: State University of New York Press, 1992], 21).

[39] For further discussion of the related distinction between a "problem" and a "mystery," see Verkamp, *Senses of Mystery*, 6, 15,n54,52.

[40] See Pieper, *Leisure*, 120; Verkamp, *Senses of Mystery*, 116, 119, 135.

[41] See Miller, *Throe of Wonder*, 3, 35.

[42] *Ibid.*, 16, 23.

[43] *Ibid.*, 21.

[44] Lonergan, *Insight*, 173–174, 9–10.

[45] Miller, *Wonder*, 33.

[46] *Ibid.*

[47] *Ibid.*, 34.

[48] *Ibid.*, 35.

[49] *Ibid.*

[50] *Ibid.*, 35–38.

[51] *Ibid.*, 37.

[52] *Ibid.*, 41.

[53] *Ibid.*, 42.

[54] *Ibid.*, 42, 45, 47, 49.

[55] *Ibid.*, 43–44.

[56] *Ibid.*, 49.

[57] *Ibid.*, 51.

[58] *Ibid.*, 50, 49–52.

[59] See Verkamp, *Evolution*, 10.

[60] Miller, *Wonder*, 35, 44.

[61] Kierkegaard, *Three Discourses on Imagined Occasions*, as cited in Miller, *Wonder*, viii.

[62] See *Supra*, Chapter Four.

[63] Plato, *Symposium*, *GB* 7:149–150.

[64] *Ibid.* See also: Pieper, *Leisure*, 77.

[65] Pieper, *Leisure*, 99.

[66] *Ibid.*, 98–99.

[67] *Ibid.*, 100.

[68] *Ibid.*, 100, 88.

[69] *Ibid.*, 88.

[70] *Ibid.*

[71] Plato, *Theaetetus*, 155: *GB* 7:519.

[72] Aristotle, *Metaphysics*, Bk I, 2, 982b: *GB* 8:500.

[73] Thomas Aquinas, *Commentary on the Metaphysics* I, 3, as cited in Pieper, *Leisure*, 69, 74.

[74] Pieper, *Leisure*, 112–116.

[75] *Ibid.*, 113, 114.

[76] Aristotle, *Metaphysics*, BK I, 2: 982f: *GB* 8:501.

[77] Plato, *Philebus* x, 16, as cited in Pieper, *Leisure*, 114, 117.

[78] Pieper, *Leisure*, 114.

[79] *Ibid.*

[80] *Ibid.*

[81] *Ibid.*, 115.

[82] See Soren Kierkegaard, *The Concept of Irony* (New York: Harper and Row, 1965), 131–138.

[83] Pieper, *Leisure*, 113.

[84] See Mircea Eliade, *Myth and Reality* (New York and Evanston: Harper and Row, 1963), 149. See also: Verkamp, *Evolution of Religion*, 123–124,n112.

[85] Pieper, *Leisure*, 113. Typical in this regard was the conclusion drawn by J. Burnet to the effect that by championing a new positivistic type of thinking, the early Ionian philosophers (or physicists) introduced a radical discontinuity between *mythos* and *logos* (J. Burnet, *Early Greek Philosophy* [London, 1920], v; Jean Pierre Vernant, *Myth and Thought Among the Greeks* [London: Routledge and Kegan Paul, 1983], 343).

[86] Eliade, *Myth and Reality*, 111, 148, 151–157; Verkamp, *Evolution*, 124n113.

[87] Pieper, *Leisure*, 113. While F. M. Cornford reemphasized the continuity between *mythos* and *logos* in ancient Greek thought by calling attention to the epistemological categories common to both (see *From Religion to Philosophy* [New York: Harper and Row, 1957] and *Principium Sapientiae, The Origins of Greek Philosophical Thought* [New York: Harper and Row, 1965]), he has also been accused of having reduced the articulations in myth and speculation about the mystery of human existence to nothing but tribal custom, and to that extent to have left unaccounted for the mystery at the very core of tribal custom itself (see Indra Kagis McEwen, *Socrates' Ancestor* [Cambridge: The MIT Press, 1997], 3). McEwen, it may be added, gives a lot of credit to Martin Heidegger and Eric Voegelin for having mitigated the picture of early Greek thinkers as either highly evolved tribesmen (as Cornford seemed to imply) or as underdeveloped nuclear physicists (as Burnet seemed to suggest) by trying to disclose early Greek thinking "as the West's first articulation of [the mystery of human existence] *as* a mystery" (Ibid.) As our earlier discussion makes clear, without a sense of mystery, there is, of course, no sense of wonder.

[88] For a few examples of the Stoic motto "*me thaumazein (nil admirari)*," see Cicero, *Tusculuan Disputations* (Cambridge and London: Harvard University Press and William Heinemann, Ltd., 1960), III, XIV, p. 263; *Horace the Epistles*, translated by Colin Macleod (Edizioni Dell'Ateneo, 1986), *Epistle* 6, p. 17; Marcus Aurelius, *Meditations* VIII, 15: *GB* 12: 286; XII, 1: *GB* 12: 307; see also Arendt, *Thinking*, 152, 248,n.66.

[89] See Verkamp, *Senses of Mystery*, 1–17.

Abbreviations

DPP   *Dictionary of Philosophy and Psychology*. Edited by James Mark Baldwin. Gloucester, MA.: Peter Smith, 1960

EP   *Encyclopedia of Philosophy*. Edited by Paul Edwards. New York: Macmillan and Co., and The Free Press, 1967.

ER   *Encyclopedia of Religion*. Edited by Mircea Eliade. New York: Macmillan, 1987.

GB   *Great Books of the Western World*. Edited by R.M Hutchins. Chicago: Encyclopedia Britannica, 1952.

IESS   *International Encyclopedia of the Social Sciences*. Edited by David L. Sills. N.P.: The Macmillan Company and The Free Press, 1968.

NCE   *New Catholic Encyclopedia*. Edited by W. J. McDonald. New York: McGraw-Hill, 1967.

Bibliography

Adams, Robert Merrihew. *Leibniz, Determinist, Theist, Idealist*. New York and Oxford: Oxford University Press, 1994.

Allen, Gay Wilson. "A New Look at Emerson and Science." In *Critical Essays on Ralph Waldo Emerson*. See Burkholder, Robert E.

Alston, William P. *Perceiving God*. Ithaca and London. Cornell University Press, 1991.

Angeles, Peter A. *Dictionary of Philosophy*. New York: Harper and Row, 1981.

Arendt, Hannah. *The Life of the Mind*. Volume One. *Thinking*. New York and London: Harcourt Brace Jovanovich, 1978.

Aristotle. *Metaphysics*. Volume 8 of *Great Books of the Western World*. See Abbreviations.

Aristotle. *Rhetoric*. Volume 9 of *Great Books of the Western World*. See Abbreviations.

Aurelius, Marcus. *Meditations*. Volume 12 of *Great Books of the Western World*. See Abbreviations

Baillie, John. *The Interpretation of Religion*. New York: Charles Scribner's Sons, 1928.

Baillie, John. *The Sense of the Presence of God*. New York: Charles Scribner's Sons, 1962.

Barth, Robert. *Coleridge and Christian Doctrine*. Cambridge: Harvard University Press, 1969.

Beardsworth, Timothy. *A Sense of Presence*. Oxford: The Religious Experience Research Unit, 1977.

Bercholz, Samuel and Kohn, Sherab Chodzin, eds. Entering the Stream: *An Introduction to the Buddha and his Teachings*. Boston: Shambhala, 1993.

Bertalanffy L. von, and Rapoport, A., ed. *General Systems*. Ann Arbor: Society of General Systems Research, 1962.

Bovet, Pierre. *The Child's Religion*. New York: E .P. Dutton and Co, 1928.

Brinton, H. *The Mystic Will*. New York: Macmillan, 1930.

Broad, C. D. *Leibniz, An Introduction*. London: Cambridge University Press, 1975.

Burkholder, Robert E. and Myerson, Joel. *Critical Essays on Ralph Waldo Emerson*. Boston: G.K. Hall and Co., 1983.

Busch, Ernst. *Goethes Religion*. Tuebingen: Furche-Verlag, 1949.

Carr, Ann. "Starting with the Human." In *A World of Grace*, 17–30. See O'Donovan, Leo J.

Cassirer, Ernst. *An Essay on Man*. New Haven: Yale University Press, 1956.

Cassirer, Ernst. *Language and Myth*. New York: Dover Publications, Inc., 1946.

Cassirer, Ernst. *The Philosophy of Symbolic Forms*, Volume 2: *Mythic Thought*. New Haven and London: Yale University Press, 1955.

Cassirer, H. W. *A Commentary on Kant's Critique of Judgment*. New York and London: Barnes and Noble, Inc., and Methuen and Co., Ltd., 1970.

Cicero. *Selected Works of Cicero*. New York: The Classics Club, 1948.

Cicero. *Tusculan-Disputations*. London: W. Heinemann, 1927.

Cicero. *Tusculan-Disputations*. Cambridge and London: Harvard University Press and William Heinemann, Ltd., 1960.

Coburn, Kathleen. *Coleridge: A Collection of Critical Essays*. Englewood-Cliffs, NJ: Prentice-Hall, Inc., 1967.

Cooper, David E. "Innateness: Old and New." *The Philosophical Review* LXXXI (October, 1972): 465–483.

Copleston, Frederick. *A History of Philosophy I, Greece and Rome*, Part II. Garden City, NY: Doubleday, 1962.

Copleston, Frederick. *A History of Philosophy II, Mediaeval Philosophy* II. Garden City, NY: Doubleday and Company, Inc., 1962.

Copleston, Frederick. *A History of Philosophy IV, Modern Philosophy*: *Descartes to Leibniz*. Garden City, NY: Doubleday, 1963.

Copleston, Frederick. *A History of Philosophy VI, Modern Philosophy*, Part II: *Kant*. Garden City, NY: Doubleday, 1964.

Coreth, Emerich. *Metaphysics*. New York: Herder and Herder, 1968.

Cornford, Francis M. *From Religion to Philosophy*. New York: Harper and Row, 1957.

Cornford, Francis M. *Principium Sapientiae, The Origins of Greek Philosophical Thought*. New York: Harper and Row, 1965.

Cottingham, John. *A Descartes Dictionary*. Oxford: Blackwell, 1993.

Cottrell, Alan P. *Goethe's View of Evil*. Edinburgh: Floris Books, 1982.

Cushman, R. E. and Grislis, E., eds. *The Heritage of Christian Thought.* New York: Harper and Row, 1965.

Davidson, Robert F. *Rudolf Otto's Interpretation of Religion.* Princeton: Princeton University Press, 1947.

Day, Martin S. *History of English Literature, 1660–1837.* Garden City, NY: Doubleday and Company, Inc., 1963.

Descartes, Rene. *Discourse on Method.* Volume 31 of *Great Books of the Western World.* See Abbreviations.

Descartes, Rene. *Meditations.* Volume 31 of *Great Books of the Western World.* See Abbreviations.

Descartes, Rene. *Notes Against a Programme.* In *The Philosophical Works of Descartes.*

Descartes, Rene. *Oeuvres de Descartes.* Paris: Librairie Philosophique J. Vrin, 1969.

Descartes, Rene. *The Passions of the Soul.* Indianapolis: Hackett Publishing Company, 1989.

Descartes, Rene. *The Philosophical Writings of Descartes III, Correspondence.* Cambridge: Cambridge University Press, 1984.

Descartes, Rene. *Principles of Philosophy.* In *The Philosophical Works of Descartes.*

Descartes, Rene. *Rules for Direction.* Volume 31 of *Great Books of the Western World.* See Abbreviations.

Descartes, Rene. *The Search after Truth.* In *The Philosophical Works of Descartes.*

Dickens, Robert. *Thoreau: The Complete Individualist.* New York: Exposition Press, 1974.

Diogenes Laertius. *Lives of Eminent Philosophers.* London: W. Heinemann, 1965.

Donceel, Joseph F. *Philosophical Anthropology.* New York: Sheed and Ward, 1967.

Donceel, Joseph F. "Transcendental Thomism." *The Monist* 58 (1974): 67–85.

Eccles, John C. "Cultural Evolution versus Biological Evolution." *Zygon*: Volume 8, 3–4 (1973).

Eccles, John C. *Evolution of the Brain: Creation of the Self.* London and New York: Routledge, 1989.

Eccles, John C. *The Human Psyche.* Berlin: Springer International, 1980.

Eliade, Mircea. *Myth and Reality.* New York and Evanston: Harper and Row, 1963.

Elkind, David. "The Development of Religious Understanding in Children and Adolescents." In *Research on Religious Development*, 656–685. See Strommen, Merton P.

Emmet, Dorothy, M. "Coleridge on the Growth of the Mind." In *Coleridge: A Collection of Critical Essays*. See Coburn, Kathleen.

Epictetus. *The Discourses of Epictetus*. Volume 12 of *Great Books of the Western World*. See Abbreviations.

Foster, Michael B. *Mystery and Philosophy*. London: SCM Press, LTD, 1957.

Fowler, James. *Stages of Faith*. San Francisco: Harper and Row, 1981.

Fries, Jakob Friedrich. *Dialogues on Morality and Religion*. Totowa, NY: Barnes and Noble, 1982.

Gavin, Carney, and others, eds. *The Word: Readings in Theology*. New York: P. J. Kenedy and Sons, 1964.

Giussani, Luigi. *The Religious Sense*. Montreal: McGill-Queens University Press, 1998.

Godin, Guy. "La notion d'admiration." *Laval Theologique et Philosophique* XVII.1 (1961).

Goldman, Ronald. *Religious Thinking From Childhood to Adolescence*. New York: The Seabury Press, 1968.

Gregory, Richard L., ed. *Oxford Companion of the Mind*. Oxford and New York: Oxford University Press, 1987.

Guenther, Herbert V. "Levels of Understanding in Buddhism." *Journal of American Oriental Society* 78.1 (January–March, 1958): 18–28.

Harrison, Peter. *'Religion' and the Religions in the English Enlightenment*. Cambridge: Cambridge University Press, 1990.

Hartner, Willy. "Goethe and the Natural Sciences." In *Goethe's View of Evil*. See Lange, Victor.

Herbert, Edward, Lord of Cherbury. *De Veritate*. Bristol: J. W. Arrowsmith, Ltd., 1937.

Hick, John. *Faith and Knowledge*. Ithaca and London: Cornell University Press, 1970.

Hick, John. *An Interpretation of Religion*. New Haven: Yale University Press, 1989.

Hirsch, E. D. Jr. *Wordsworth and Schelling*. New Haven: Yale University Press, 1960.

Horace. *The Epistles*. Edizioni Dell'Ateneo, 1986.

James, William. *Principles of Psychology*. Volume 53 of *Great Books of the Western World*. See Abbreviations.

James, William. *The Varieties of Religious Experience*. New York: New American Library, 1958.

Jung, Carl G. *The Archetypes and the Collective Unconscious*. In *The Collected Works of C.G. Jung*, Volume 9, Part I. Princeton: Princeton University Press, 1959.

Jung, Carl G. *Man and his Symbols*. New York: Doubleday, 1964.

Kant, Immanuel. *The Critique of Judgement*. Volume 42 of *Great Books of the Western World*. See Abbreviations.

Kant, Immanuel. *The Critique of Pure Reason*. Volume 42 of *Great Books of the Western World*. See Abbreviations.

Kierkegaard, Soren. *The Concept of Irony*. New York: Harper and Row, 1965.

Klubertanz, G.P. "Estimative Power." *NCE* 5:558.

Klubertanz, G.P. *The Discursive Power*. Saint Louis: The Modern Schoolman, 1952.

Knasas, John F. X. "Intellectual Dynamism in Transcendental Thomism: A Metaphysical Assessment." *American Catholic Philosophical Quarterly* LXIX, no. 1 (1995): 15–28.

Koehler, Wolfgang. *The Task of Gestalt Psychology*. Princeton: Princeton University Press, 1969.

Kohlberg, Lawrence. *The Philosophy of Moral Development*. San Francisco: Harper and Row, 1981.

Kottich, R.G. *Die Lehre von den angeborenen Ideen seit Herbert von Cherbury*. Berlin: Verlagsbuchhandlung von Richard Schoetz, 1917.

Kress, Robert. *A Rahner Handbook*. Atlanta: John Knox Press, 1982.

Lange, Victor. ed. *Goethe: A Collection of Critical Essays*. Englewood Cliffs, NJ: Prentice-Hall, Inc., 1968.

Langer, Suzanne. *Philosophy in a New Key*. New York: The New American Library, 1953.

Leibniz, G. W. *New Essays Concerning Human Understanding*. New York: Macmillan, 1896.

Leibniz, G. W. *New Essays on Human Understanding*. Cambridge: Cambridge University Press, 1996.

Leibniz, G. W. *Philosophical Papers and Letters*. Chicago: The University of Chicago Press, 1996.

Levy-Bruhl, Lucien. *Primitive Mentality*. Boston: Beacon Press, 1966.

Lindbeck, George A. "The *A Priori* in St. Thomas' Theory of Knowledge." In *The Heritage of Christian Thought*, 41–63. See Cushman R. E.

Lonergan, Bernard J. F. *Collection.* New York: Herder and Herder, 1967.

Lonergan, Bernard J. F. *Insight, A Study of Human Understanding.* London, New York, and Toronto: Longmans, Green and Co., 1958.

Lonergan, Bernard J. F. *Method in Theology.* Toronto: University of Toronto Press, 1990.

Lonergan, Bernard J. F. *Philosophy of God, and Theology.* Philadelphia: The Westminster Press, 1973.

Lonergan, Bernard J. F. *A Second Collection.* London: Darton, Longman and Todd, 1974.

Lonergan, Bernard J. F. *Understanding and Being.* New York and Toronto: The Edwin Mellen Press, 1980.

Lorenz, Konrad. *Evolution and Modification of Behavior.* Chicago: The University of Chicago Press, 1967.

Lorenz, Konrad. "Kant's Doctrine of the A Priori in the Light of Contemporary Biology." In *General Systems*, 23–35. See von Bertalanffy.

Loy, David. *Nonduality: A Study in Comparative Philosophy.* New Haven and London: Yale University Press, 1988.

Lumsden, Charles and Wilson, Edward O. *Genes, Mind, and Culture.* Cambridge: Harvard University Press, 1981.

Marechal, Joseph. *A Marechal Reader.* New York: Herder and Herder, 1970.

Marty, Martin E., and Peerman, Dean G. *A Handbook of Christian Theologians.* Cleveland and New York: The World Publishing Company, 1967.

McCool, Gerald A. "The Philosophy of the Human Person in Karl Rahner's Theology." *Theological Studies* XXII (1961): 537–62.

McDougall, William. *An Introduction to Social Psychology.* Boston: John W. Luce and Co., 1926.

McEwen, Indra Kagis. *Socrates' Ancestor, An Essay on Architectural Beginnings.* Cambridge: MIT Press, 1997.

McRae, Robert. *Leibniz: Perception, Apperception, and Thought.* Toronto and Buffalo: University of Toronto Press, 1976.

Meynell, Hugo A. *An Introduction to the Philosophy of Bernard Lonergan.* Toronto and Buffalo: University of Toronto Press, 1991.

Midgley, Mary. *Beast and Man, The Roots of Human Nature.* Ithaca, NY: Cornell University Press, 1978.

Miller, Jerome. *In the Throe of Wonder: Intimations of the Sacred in a Post-Modern World.* Albany, NY: State University of New York Press, 1992.

Moore, Charles A., ed. *Essays in East-West Philosophy.* Honolulu: University of Hawaii Press, 1951.

Morris, John M., ed. *Descartes Dictionary.* New York: Philosophical Library, 1971.

Munsey, Brenda, ed. *Moral Development, Moral Education, and Kohlberg.* Birmingham, Ala.: Religious Education Press, 1980.

Murti, R. R. V. *The Central Philosophy of Buddhism: A Study of the Madhyamika System.* London: George Allen and Unwin, Ltd., 1968.

Newman, John Henry. *Grammar of Assent.* Garden City, NY: Doubleday and Company, Inc., 1955.

Niebuhr, Richard. "Friedrich Schleiermacher." In *A Handbook of Christian Theologians.* See Marty, Martin E.

Niebuhr, Richard. *Schleiermacher on Christ and Religion.* New York: Charles Scribner's Sons, 1964.

Nisbet, H. B. *Goethe and the Scientific Tradition.* London: Institute of Germanic Studies, 1972.

Noss, David S. and Noss, John B. *A History of the World's Religions.* New York and London: Macmillan, 1990.

Nowell-Smith, P. H. *Ethics.* London: Penguin Books, Ltd.

O'Donovan, Leo J., ed. *A World of Grace.* New York: Crossroad, 1989.

Otto, Rudolf. *Das Gefuehl des Ueberweltlichen.* Muenchen: C.H. Beck'sche Verlagsbuchhandlung, 1932.

Otto, Rudolf. *The Idea of the Holy.* New York: Oxford University Press, 1958.

Otto, Rudolf. *Naturalism and Religion.* London: Williams and Norgate, 1913.

Otto, Rudolf. *The Philosophy of Religion.* London: Williams and Norgate, 1931.

Otto, Rudolf. *Religious Essays.* London: Oxford University Press, 1931.

Pascal, Blaise. *Pensees and other writings.* Oxford: Oxford University Press, 1995.

Peterson, Michael; Hasker, William; Reichenbach, Bruce; Bassinger, David. *Reason and Religious Belief.* New York and Oxford: Oxford University Press, 1998.

Piaget, Jean. *Biology and Knowledge.* Chicago and London: University of Chicago Press, 1971.

Piaget, Jean. *The Child's Conception of the World*. Totowa, N.J.: Rowman and Littlefield, 1983.

Piaget, Jean. *The Moral Judgment of the Child*. New York: The Free press, 1965.

Piaget, Jean. *The Origins of Intelligence in Children*. New York: International Universities Press, 1975.

Piaget, Jean. *The Principles of Genetic Epistemology*. London: Routledge and Kegan Paul, 1972.

Piattelli-Palmarini, Massimo, ed. *Language and Learning, The Debate Between Jean Piaget and Noam Chomsky*. Cambridge: Harvard University Press, 1980.

Pieper, Josef. *Leisure, The Basis of Culture*. New York and Toronto: The New American Library, 1963.

Plato. *Meno, The Republic, The Symposium, Theaetetus*. Volume 7 of *Great Books of the Western World*. See Abbreviations.

Potter, Vincent G. "'Vaguely like a Man': The Theism of Charles S. Peirce." In *God Knowable and Unknowable*, 241–254. See Roth, Robert J.

Preus, J. Samuel. *Explaining Religion*. New Haven and London: Yale University Press, 1987.

Proudfoot, Wayne. *Religious Experience*. Berkeley: University of California Press, 1985.

Rahner, Karl. *Christian at the Crossroads*. New York: The Seabury Press, 1975.

Rahner, Karl. *Foundations of Christian Faith*. New York: The Seabury Press, 1978.

Rahner, Karl. "Priest and Poet." In *The Word: Readings in Theology*, 3–26. See Gavin, Carney.

Rahner, Karl. *A Rahner Reader*. New York: The Seabury Press, 1975.

Rahner, Karl. *Spirit in the World*. New York: Herder and Herder, 1967.

Rahner, Karl and Vorgrimler, Herbert. *Theological Dictionary*. New York: Herder and Herder, 1965.

Rahner, Karl. *Theological Investigations IV.* London: Darton, Longman, and Todd, 1966.

Regis, L. M. *Epistemology*. New York: The Macmillan Company.

Reiser, William E. "Lonergan's Notion of the Religious Apriori." *The Thomist* XXXV, no. 2 (April, 1971): 247–258.

Richards, Robert J. *Darwin and the Emergence of Evolutionary Theories of Mind and Behavior*. Chicago: The University of Chicago Press, 1987.

Richards, Robert J. "Influence of Sensationalist Tradition on Early Theories of the Evolution of Behavior." *Journal of the History of Ideas* 40 (1979): 85–105.

Richards, Robert J. "The Innate and Learned: The Evolution of Konrad Lorenz's Theory of Instinct." *Philosophy of the Social Sciences* 4 (1974): 111–133.

Richardson, Robert D., Jr. *Henry Thoreau: A Life of the Mind.* Berkeley: University of California Press, 1986.

Riet, Georges Van. *Thomistic Epistemology.* St. Louis and London: B. Herder Book Co., 1963.

Roth, Robert J., ed. *God Knowable and Unknowable.* New York: Fordham University Press, 1973.

Royce, James E. *Man and Meaning.* New York: McGraw-Hill, Inc., 1969.

Ruland, Richard, ed. *Twentieth Century Interpretations of Walden.* Englewood Cliffs, NJ: Prentice-Hall, Inc., 1968.

Ruse, Michael. *The Darwinian Paradigm: Essays on its history, philosophy, and religious implications.* London and New York: Routledge, 1989.

Ruse, Michael. *Taking Darwin Seriously.* Oxford: Basil Blackwell, 1986.

Sala, Giovanni. "The *A Priori* in Human Knowledge: Kant's *Critique of Pure Reason* and Lonergan's *Insight.*" *The Thomist* XL, No. 2 (April, 1976): 179–221.

Schleiermacher, Friedrich. *On Religion, Speeches to its Cultured Despisers.* New York: Harper and Row, 1958.

Schofield, Edmund A. and Baron, Robert C., eds. *Thoreau's World and Ours.* Golden, CO: North American Press, 1993.

Sdorow, Lester M. *Psychology.* Madison, Wisc.: Brown and Benchmark, 1993.

Seligman, Martin E. P., and Hager, Joanne L. *Biological Boundaries of Learning.* New York: Appleton-Century-Crofts, 1972.

Sheehan, Thomas. *Karl Rahner: The Philosophical Foundations.* Athens: Ohio University Press, 1987.

Skinner, Charles E. and Harriman, Philip L., eds. *Child Psychology: Child Development and Modern Education.* New York: Macmillan, 1941.

Smith, J. J. "Religious Development of Children." In *Child Psychology: Child Development and Modern Education*, 273–98. See Skinner, Charles E.

Stich, Stephen P. *Innate Ideas*. Berkeley, Los Angeles, and London: University of California Press, 1975.

Streng, Frederick J. *Emptiness*. Nashville and New York: Abingdon Press, 1967.

Strommen, Merton P., ed. *Research on Religious Development*. New York: Hawthorn Books, 1971.

Suzuki, Daisetz Teitaro. "Reason and Intuition in Buddhist Philosophy" In *Essays in East-West Philosophy*, 17–48. See Moore, Charles A.

Suzuki, D. T. *Zen Buddhism: Selected Writings*. New York: Doubleday, 1996.

Swinburne, Richard. *The Evolution of the Soul*. Oxford: Clarendon Press, 1986.

Swinburne, Richard. *The Existence of God*. Oxford: Clarendon Press, 1989.

Taylor, A. E. *Plato: The Man and His Work*. New York: The Dial Press, 1936.

Thomas Aquinas, *The Summa Theologica*. Volume 19 of *Great Books of the Western World*. See Abbreviations.

Thorpe, W. H. *Learning and Instinct in Animals*. London: Methuen and Co., 1956.

Verkamp, Bernard J. *The Evolution of Religion: A Re-examination*. Scranton: The University of Scranton Press, 1995.

Verkamp, Bernard J. "Hick's Interpretation of Religious Pluralism." *International Journal for the Philosophy of Religion* 30(1991): 103–124.

Verkamp, Bernard J. *The Senses of Mystery: Religious and Non-Religious*. Scranton: The University of Scranton Press, 1997.

Vernant, Jean Pierre. *Myth and Thougth among the Greeks*. London: Routledge and Kegan Paul, 1983.

Wach, Joachim. *Sociology of Religion*. Chicago and London: The University of Chicago Press, 1967.

Wahr, Frederick B. *Emerson and Goethe*. Folcroft, PA: The Folcroft Press, Inc., 1969.

Webb, Eugene. *Philosophers of Consciousness*. Seattle and London: University of Washington Press, 1988.

Weger, Karl-Heinz. *Karl Rahner: An Introduction to His Theology*. New York: Seabury Press, 1980.

Wilson, E. O. *On Human Nature*. Cambridge: Harvard University Press, 1978.

Wilson, E. O. *Sociobiology: The New Synthesis*. Cambridge: Belknap Press, 1975.

Wilson, Patricia. "Human Knowledge of God's Existence in the Theology of Bernard Lonergan." *The Thomist* XXXV, No. 2 (April, 1971): 259–275.

Worgul, George S. "The Ghost of Newman in Lonergan Corpus." *The Modern Schoolman* LIV (May, 1977): 317–332.

Wright, William K. "The Genesis of the Categories." *The Journal of Philosophy, Psychology and Scientific Methods* X. 24 (November 20, 1913): 645–657.

Yolton, John W. *John Locke and the Way of Ideas*. Oxford: Oxford University Press, 1956.

Young, J. Z. *Philosophy and the Brain*. Oxford and New York: Oxford University Press, 1987.

INDEX

121